Urban Change and Regional Development at the Margins of Europe

Evaluating the Effects of the EU Policy

Edited by
Ignazio Vinci and Paula Russell

LONDON AND NEW YORK

First published 2023
by Routledge
4 Park Square, Milton Park, Abingdon, Oxon, OX14 4RN

and by Routledge
605 Third Avenue, New York, NY 10158

Routledge is an imprint of the Taylor & Francis Group, an informa business

© 2023 Taylor & Francis

All rights reserved. No part of this book may be reprinted or reproduced or utilised in any form or by any electronic, mechanical, or other means, now known or hereafter invented, including photocopying and recording, or in any information storage or retrieval system, without permission in writing from the publishers.

Trademark notice: Product or corporate names may be trademarks or registered trademarks, and are used only for identification and explanation without intent to infringe.

British Library Cataloguing-in-Publication Data
A catalogue record for this book is available from the British Library

ISBN13: 978-1-032-28048-6 (hbk)
ISBN13: 978-1-032-28050-9 (pbk)
ISBN13: 978-1-003-29509-9 (ebk)

DOI: 10.4324/9781003295099

Typeset in Minion Pro
by codeMantra

Publisher's Note
The publisher accepts responsibility for any inconsistencies that may have arisen during the conversion of this book from journal articles to book chapters, namely the inclusion of journal terminology.

Disclaimer
Every effort has been made to contact copyright holders for their permission to reprint material in this book. The publishers would be grateful to hear from any copyright holder who is not here acknowledged and will undertake to rectify any errors or omissions in future editions of this book.

Urban Change and Regional Development at the Margins of Europe

Since the beginning of the 1990s, regions and urban areas have become a primary target of EU Cohesion Policy. For a number of European cities, especially in the less developed regions, this has resulted in a unique opportunity for the implementation of extensive development projects, as well as delivering innovations in urban policy and local governance.

Through the detailed observation of planning processes which took place in four European cities – Porto (PT), Malaga (ES), Palermo (IT), and Thessaloniki (EL) – this book explores the different ways that EU intervention can affect the policy process locally, from the regeneration of decayed neighbourhoods and the creation of key services for improving the quality of life, to the establishment of new governance relations and increasing the institutional capacity in local government.

This book also provides a critical reflection on the impact of EU urban policy in reducing regional disparities and the extent to which Cohesion Policy has helped cities to open new pathways for local development. With a special focus on the EU's marginal regions, this book is a guide to understanding how EU policy has affected urban change and local development across Europe.

The chapters in this book were originally published as a special issue of the journal *Urban Research & Practice*.

Ignazio Vinci is Professor of Urban Planning in the Department of Architecture at the University of Palermo, Italy. His research activity focuses on urban development in Europe, urban policy, spatial planning, and territorial governance. He is Vice President of the European Urban Research Association (EURA).

Paula Russell is Assistant Professor at the School of Architecture Planning and Environmental Policy at University College Dublin, Ireland. Her main area of research relates to the role of civil society in the planning process, looking at issues of engagement and influence. She is a member of the board of the European Urban Research Association (EURA) and Associate Editor of the journal *Urban Research & Practice*.

Contents

Citation Information vi
Notes on Contributors vii

Introduction 1
Ignazio Vinci and Paula Russell

1 Cities and regional disparities in the European Union: evolving geographies
   and challenges for Cohesion Policy 6
   Ignazio Vinci

2 The influence of EU policy on local policy-making, governance
   and urban change. Evidence from Porto, Portugal 28
   João Igreja and Paulo Conceição

3 Transferring sustainability: imaginaries and processes in EU funded
   projects in Thessaloniki 53
   Evangelia Athanassiou

4 Understanding the influence of EU urban policy in Spanish cities: the case
   of Málaga 75
   Sonia De Gregorio Hurtado

5 How the EU regional policy can shape urban change in
   Southern Europe: learning from different planning processes in Palermo 101
   Ignazio Vinci

Index 127

Citation Information

The chapters in this book were originally published in the *Urban Research & Practice*, volume 14, issue 4 (2021). When citing this material, please use the original page numbering for each article, as follows:

Introduction
Introduction to the special issue
Ignazio Vinci and Paula Russell
Urban Research & Practice, volume 14, issue 4 (2021) pp. 345–349

Chapter 1
Cities and regional disparities in the European Union: evolving geographies and challenges for Cohesion Policy
Ignazio Vinci
Urban Research & Practice, volume 14, issue 4 (2021) pp. 350–371

Chapter 2
The influence of EU policy on local policy-making, governance and urban change. Evidence from Porto, Portugal
João Igreja and Paulo Conceição
Urban Research & Practice, volume 14, issue 4 (2021) pp. 372–396

Chapter 3
Transferring sustainability: imaginaries and processes in EU funded projects in Thessaloniki
Evangelia Athanassiou
Urban Research & Practice, volume 14, issue 4 (2021) pp. 397–418

Chapter 4
Understanding the influence of EU urban policy in Spanish cities: the case of Málaga
Sonia De Gregorio Hurtado
Urban Research & Practice, volume 14, issue 4 (2021) pp. 419–444

Chapter 5
How the EU regional policy can shape urban change in Southern Europe: learning from different planning processes in Palermo
Ignazio Vinci
Urban Research & Practice, volume 14, issue 4 (2021) pp. 445–470

For any permission-related enquiries please visit:
http://www.tandfonline.com/page/help/permissions

Notes on Contributors

Evangelia Athanassiou, Department of Architecture, Aristotle University of Thessaloniki, Greece.

Paulo Conceição, CITTA – Centre for Research on Territory, Transports and Environment, University of Porto, Portugal.

Sonia De Gregorio Hurtado, Department of Urban and Spatial Planning, Universidad Politécnica de Madrid, España.

João Igreja, Department of Architecture, University of Palermo, Italy.

Paula Russell, University College Dublin, Ireland.

Ignazio Vinci, Department of Architecture, University of Palermo, Italy.

Introduction

Ignazio Vinci and Paula Russell

European urban policy has often been portrayed in the literature as a clear case of 'Europeanization' (Carpenter 2013; Dossi 2017; Carpenter et al. 2020; Hamedinger and Wolffhardt 2010; Marshall 2005). This concept relates to that multidirectional process whereby the reshaping of national and sub-national policies under the influence of the EU is accompanied by a bottom-up and even horizontal transfer of knowledge, paradigms and best practices, that are increasingly shared by institutions in a multi-level governance system. In this special issue we largely concentrate on the first type of relationships, the ways in which the planning practices, and local development trajectories, of certain cities are being influenced by the implementation of EU projects.

Cities started to be explicitly viewed as key elements of regional development in the European Community at the end of the 1980s. Following the reform of the Structural Funds approved in 1988, the reshaping of regional policy was accompanied by programmes that, for the first time, were specifically designed to stimulate actions in urban areas (Williams 1996). The success of these early initiatives – i.e. Urban Pilot Projects – was essential to demonstrate that the European Union could play a key role in overcoming the development problems experienced by European cities, including the social consequences of economic decline and the environmental challenges of urban areas (Atkinson and Zimmermann 2016).

As a result, the subsequent decades were earmarked by growing political and financial efforts from various EU institutions to widen the role of cities within Cohesion Policy. This was first manifested in the creation of different policy instruments directly targeted on cities (i.e. URBAN Community Initiative, URBACT or, more recently, the Urban Innovative Actions), in order to increase the capacity of municipalities to experiment with new planning solutions to face the challenges of urban development. Later, the focus on urban issues and challenges also became embedded in the mainstream instruments of Cohesion Policy, including the Structural Funds, which are the responsibility of regional authorities. This progress led to the acknowledgment that the development of cities and regions are, to some extent, inextricably linked, and to recognise that this symbiosis must be a guiding principle of any future reform of EU Cohesion Policy (McCann 2015; Medeiros 2019).

After almost 30 years of widespread interventions in cities and regions there is no clear measure to prove the impact of EU urban policies on regional development and vice versa (EC 2020; Farole, Goga, and Ionescu-Heroiu 2018). Post the 2008 economic crisis, many urban areas in Europe are still suffering with development problems and socio-economic inequalities, often accompanied by similar issues at regional and metropolitan levels (EUROSTAT 2016). At the same time, however, there is some evidence that Cohesion Policy has stimulated the progress of urban policy and the wealth of cities in many parts of Europe. In several regions that were ranked among the 'less developed' in the 1990s, the substantial EU funds that were made available for the implementation of plans and projects, have had clear impacts on urban areas. For many other cities across Europe, EU intervention has meant undertaking relevant changes to their urban structure, through the regeneration of deprived neighborhoods, the construction of modern transport infrastructures, or the creation of new facilities to increase economic attractiveness and quality of life.

Against the backdrop of these contrasting experiences, this special issue was conceived with the aim of exploring some of the different ways EU regional policy may have influenced the development process of four Southern European cities, Porto (PT), Malaga (ES), Palermo (IT), and Thessaloniki (GR). The selection of case studies here is not a coincidence, since they are all cities at the 'margins of Europe' in both the sense of places outside the geographical core of the continent and located in those regions – the 'less developed regions' – where EU Cohesion policy has been manifested in significant investment over an extended period of time. For that reason, the special issue also seeks to provide an urban perspective to regional marginality, often neglected in the debate around the urban dimension within EU Cohesion Policy.

In the case studies presented in the following articles, the authors were requested to carry out their analysis under the lens of some general research questions. The first one relates to the impact of EU projects on the physical and/or socio-economic regeneration of the city, or certain parts of the urban area where their influence is more recognisable. Another group of questions refers to the potential effect of EU initiatives on local governance, in terms of stakeholder participation in planning processes, the emergence of public–private cooperation, or new institutional arrangements and styles in government. Last but not least, authors have tried to understand whether or not European sponsored projects have delivered new planning capacities in the policy making process, and how the EU approaches and methods to encourage sustainable urban development have been embedded in local planning practices.

In these analytical efforts authors show that urban transformations may be the result of various planning initiatives – from area-based integrated action plans to more sectoral interventions (i.e. infrastructure, public facilities, etc.) –, and that the development strategies of cities can be influenced by other external factors, including national urban policies and changes in local politics. As a result, in any given city EU planning initiatives must be seen as part of a wider policy-making process, being influenced by both changes in regional and local policies, as well as by the shifting priorities of the EU in addressing urban development over the different programming cycles.

To contextualise the processes in the four cities studied, the first article of the special issue, written by Ignazio Vinci, places the emergence of an urban dimension in EU policy, within the framework of Cohesion Policy and its primary objective of reducing regional disparities. The article begins by reviewing the debate surrounding regional disparities in Europe and provides a description of the changing geography of the EU through the perspective of the different Cohesion Policy periods. The paper then traces the history of the political process that has led urban areas to become a pillar of EU regional policy culminating in the emergence of the 'sustainable urban development' concept. The different interpretations of this concept in the planning practices of contemporary European cities are then discussed. In the final part of the article, the author identifies some of the limits of EU regional policy in addressing problematic development issues in urban areas (i.e. territorial divides and social exclusion). At the same time, however, he recognises that the linkage between the urban and regional dimensions of sustainable development is expected to remain a core issue for both policy-makers and urban scholars in the near future.

In the article on the Porto case study, written by João Igreja and Paulo Conceição, the authors investigate the connections between European projects and national policies in the city's recent transformation process, with a specific focus on the regeneration of the old town. In the context of a country that has benefited significantly from EU regional policy since the 1990s, Porto emerges as one of the Portuguese cities most actively involved in the Europeanisation process, with resulting influences on both the policy-making approach and local governance. Nevertheless, after reviewing the most relevant planning episodes in the city over the preceding decades, the article stresses that the transfer of the EU approach to local urban policy has not followed a linear process and that various models of intervention have overlapped over time. By recognising the effects of EU urban initiatives during certain periods of the city's recent history, the authors arrive at the conclusion that the legacy of other political and institutional processes must not be neglected in explaining the regeneration process. This includes the neo-liberal turn that has shaped urban policy since the mid 2000s and reforms of local government.

In the study on the case of Málaga, Sonia De Gregorio Hurtado explores a Spanish city that is acknowledged as an exemplar in the use of EU funds, particularly in stimulating the revitalisation of the historic centre through area-based projects. The description of the context covers a period that starts with the beginning of the Democratic Period (1975), a wide angle perspective that is essential to understanding the way in which the innovative approaches to urban development promoted by the EU have been embedded in the praxis of national and local policy-making. In this context, by undertaking a detailed review of a range of planning initiatives, the author highlights the manner in which EU projects have been implemented hand in hand with increasing institutional capacity. This is illustrated by the key role played by the municipality in both strategic and operational terms. The in-depth analysis of the current development pattern of the historic centre shows however, that over this long-term period, the EU programmes were not able to effectively address the city's social problems and could not prevent the emergence of gentrification and a tourist-led local economy. Through the observation of these processes, the author concludes by pointing out useful lessons for the evolution of EU urban policy in the post-2020 scenario.

In a case similar to that of Málaga, Ignazio Vinci explores the role of EU programmes in the development process of Palermo (the fifth largest Italian city) through a long term and multidimensional perspective. Firstly, EU initiatives are examined in the light of relevant external factors, including the changing priorities associated with urban areas in national policies and the impact of the post-2008 crisis on local government. Secondly, the changing context of European projects in the city is also presented as a result of drastic shifts in local politics, with the emergence of different – and often contrasting – development strategies with the power to affect the targets of EU funds over time. In this article, the author argues that the effectiveness of EU projects has also been significantly influenced by the way they were implemented in terms of spatial and sectoral integration. Overall, a greater spatial and thematic concentration has turned out to be a key factor in the impact of EU projects' action plans (e.g. in the case of the old town regeneration), while the road towards sustainable development is still unclear when this objective is addressed to an urban or a metropolitan dimension.

In her paper, Evangelia Athanassiou investigates the way urban sustainability has been interpreted in the urban regeneration projects planned after the outbreak of the financial crisis (2010) in Thessaloniki, the second largest Greek city. The article starts with a critical analysis of the imaginaries, goals and processes promoted by EU urban policies, and their limits when transferred to the socio-political context of Southern Europe. More specifically, the author focuses on urban sustainability, outlining the way it is conceptualized in official EU documents. The influence of the concept of sustainability on spatial planning at national level in Greece is then explored and, in a fine-grained way, the manner in which the objective of sustainable development is embedded in urban regeneration projects is investigated. With this framework as a backdrop, various projects and integrated action plans in Thessaloniki are examined, from the Urban Pilot Project aimed at revitalizing historic districts in the city centre, to the waterfront regeneration realized during the 2007–2013 programming cycle. Through the analysis of these projects, the author shows how the urban sustainability concept can take different operational meanings in practice and, at the same time, its wide use as an instrument to legitimize the Europeanisation of local policy in the country is explained.

As awhole these papers provide insights into some of the positive impacts of Cohesion policy. They can be found both on the material infrastructure of the respective cities and on the quality of policies and practices being developed by various actors at city level. These practices also illustrate that the challenges of urban areas remain entrenched, embedded in local political and cultural contexts which, in turn, are part of much wider regional, national and global networks. This explains why the contribution of cities to regional development is so inextricable and, at the same time, that a strong focus on urban development is still needed to help future EU policy.

Disclosure statement

No potential conflict of interest was reported by the author(s).

References

Atkinson, R., and K. Zimmermann. 2016. "Cohesion Policy and Cities: An Ambivalent Relationship?" In *Handbook on Cohesion Policy in the EU*, edited by S. Piattoni and L. Polverari, 413–426. Cheltenham: Edward Elgar.

Carpenter, J. 2013. "Sustainable Urban Regeneration within the European Union: A Case of 'Europeanization'." In *The Routledge Companion to Urban Regeneration*, edited by M. E. Leary and J. McCarthy.138–147. London: Routledge.

Carpenter, J., M. Gonzalez Medina, M. A. Huete Garcia, and S. De Gregorio Hurtado. 2020. "Variegated Europeanization and Urban Policy: Dynamics of Policy Transfer in France, Italy, Spain and the UK." *European Urban and Regional Studies* 27 (3): 227–245. doi:10.1177/0969776419898508.

Dossi, S. 2017. *Cities and the European Union. Mechanisms and Modes of Europeanisation*. London: Rowman & Littlefield International.

EC – European Commission. 2020. *Seventh Report on Economic, Social and Territorial Cohesion*. Luxembourg: Office for Official Publications of the European Communities.

EUROSTAT. 2016. *Urban Europe. Statistics on Cities, Towns and Suburbs*. Luxembourg: Publications Office of the European Union.

Farole, T., S. Goga, and M. Ionescu-Heroiu. 2018. *Rethinking Lagging Regions: Using Cohesion Policy to Deliver on the Potential of Europe's Regions*. Washington: World Bank.

Hamedinger, A., and A. Wolffhardt. 2010. *The Europeanization of Cities: Policies, Urban Change and Urban Networks*. Amsterdam: Techne Press.

Marshall, A. 2005. "Europeanization at the Urban Level: Local Actors, Institutions." *Journal of European Public Policy* 12 (4): 668–686. doi:10.1080/13501760500160292.

McCann, P. 2015. *The Regional and Urban Policy of the European Union*. Cheltenham: Elgar Publishing.

Medeiros, E. ed. 2019. *Territorial Cohesion. The Urban Dimension*. Verlag: Springer.

Williams, R. H. 1996. *European Union Spatial Policy and Planning*. London: Paul Chapman Publishing.

Cities and regional disparities in the European Union: evolving geographies and challenges for Cohesion Policy

Ignazio Vinci

ABSTRACT
Since the nineties, urban areas have assumed a growing importance in EU Cohesion Policy. This process, which is being implemented through various political steps and policy instruments, has led cities to be recognised as key elements in the promotion of balanced development. After decades of planning experiments at different territorial scales, however, the extent to which EU urban policy has contributed to regional development is currently under debate. This paper seeks to describe the evolution of the urban dimension within EU Cohesion Policy, with a focus on the role of cities in those countries and regions experiencing development problems.

1. Introduction

Since the end of the eighties, regions and urban areas have been viewed as key elements of territorial development in the European Community (EC). Following the introduction of the European Regional Development Fund in the mid-1970s, a milestone in this process was the 1988 reform of European Structural Funds, after which European regional policy was radically reshaped according to a series of new principles including: firstly, a clearer identification of the 'lagging regions'[1] where EC support should be mainly addressed and, secondly, an extensive 'integrated approach' to planning in order to focus on multiple development objectives at regional and local levels (Brunazzo 2016).[2]

The other considerable effect of the 1988 reform lies in the recognition of the role cities (and urban policy) can play in the regional development process and, therefore, in the reduction of regional disparities. As a result, through a process supported by the growing political and financial commitment of various EU institutions,[3] from the early 1990s the space for urban initiatives within Cohesion Policy has grown substantially in different directions (Atkinson 2015; Atkinson and Zimmermann 2016; Cotella 2019; Hamedinger and Wolffhardt 2010). These efforts have led to an acknowledgement of the development of cities and regions as two elements of the same question, and a recognition that urban development is a relevant policy challenge that remains at the heart of the latest Cohesion Policy reforms (Barca 2009; Bachtler et al. 2017; Dijkstra, Garcilazo, and McCann 2013; McCann 2015; Medeiros 2019; Piattoni and Polverari. 2016).

Table 1. Weight of the less-developed regions by country after East Germany entrance in the EU (1990).

Country	Population	Number of LDRs (on total)	Extent of LDRs (% Country Area)	Weight of LDRs (% Population)
Germany	63,163,158	5 (36)	30.2	23.5
Italy	57,661,000	8 (20)	40.8	36.8
United Kingdom	57,366,085	1 (35)	5.8	2.8
France	56,735,000	5 (26)	17.9	3.0
Spain	38,868,830	10 (18)	71.0	52.4
Greece	10,160,689	13 (13)	100.0	100.0
Portugal	9,840,897	7 (7)	100.0	100.0
Ireland	3,513,645	1 (1)	100.0	100.0

Author's elaboration on EUROSTAT data.

Table 2. Weight of the less developed regions by country in 2014.

Country	Population	Number of LDRs (of total)	Extent of LDRs (% Country Area)	Weight of LDRs (% Population)
France	66,165,980	5 (27)	14.0	3.2
United Kingdom	64,351,203	2 (40)	6.9	3.9
Italy	60,782,668	5 (21)	27.9	28.9
Spain	46,512,199	1 (19)	8.2	2.4
Poland	38,017,856	15 (16)	88.6	86.0
Romania	19,947,311	7 (8)	99.2	88.5
Portugal	10,427,301	5 (7)	90.4	66.2
Greece	10,926,807	6 (13)	53.0	41.0
Czech Republic	10,512,419	7 (8)	99.4	88.1
Hungary	9,877,365	6 (7)	92.6	69.7
Bulgaria	7,245,677	6 (6)	100.0	100.0
Slovakia	5,415,949	3 (4)	95.8	88.5
Croatia	4,246,809	2 (2)	100.0	100.0
Lithuania	2,943,472	1 (1)	100.0	100.0
Slovenia	2,061,085	1 (2)	61.3	53.0
Latvia	2,001,468	1 (1)	100.0	100.0
Estonia	1,315,819	1 (1)	100.0	100.0

Author's elaboration on EUROSTAT data.

After three decades of extensive intervention on cities and regions, however, there is no clear evidence of the impact of EU urban policies on regional development and vice versa. Different analyses have recognised positive feedback in some countries and programming periods (EC – European Commission 2006, 2009; EP – European Parliament 2005, 2014), but the role played by EU regional policy on the reduction of socio-economic inequalities within and among urban areas remains unclear. This is further demonstrated by the fact – as illustrated in section 3 of this paper – that regional disparities are found in both more and less urbanised countries in Europe (EUROSTAT 2016; EC – European Commission 2016).

At the same time, we also need to acknowledge that Cohesion Policy has stimulated the urban policy process in many parts of Europe. In several less developed regions, substantial EU funds were made available by regional authorities for the implementation of projects with various impacts on the urban dimension (Ramsden and Colini 2013). For many cities across Europe, this has meant undertaking relevant change processes through the regeneration of deprived neighborhoods, the construction of modern mobility infrastructures, or new facilities to increase urban attractiveness or the quality of life.

Against the background of such a mixed picture, this paper acts as a framework for the case studies presented in the special issue 'Urban change and regional development at the margins of Europe', which seeks to analyse the different role played by EU regional policy in the development process of four Southern European cities (Porto, Malaga, Palermo, and Thessaloniki). Looking at the different ways these cities have dealt with urban issues in the context of the EU approach to regional development, this paper provides a territorial perspective on regional disparities and a description of the process that has led the urban dimension to be addressed within EU Cohesion Policy.

The paper is structured as follows: After this introduction, in section two the debate relating to regional disparities in the European Union is briefly reviewed, and the way urban areas are viewed in literature as part of the regional development process. In the third section, the changing geography of the EU from the perspective of Cohesion Policy is described, with a focus on the importance of cities in the lagging regions. The fourth section provides an overview of the political process that has led urban initiatives to become a pillar of EU regional policy together with an analysis of the different interpretations of the concept of 'sustainable urban development' in different planning contexts. Finally, with a view to the challenges faced by cities in the post-2020 period, in the last section we outline the limits and potential of EU regional policy in addressing some relevant development issues in urban areas.

2. The changing geography of regional disparities under the lens of Cohesion Policy

Cohesion Policy was initially conceived as a distributive instrument to improve the economic performances of the poorest regions and, through that, to reducing disparities among European countries (Leonardi 2005). In that perspective, based on a classical economic approach to regional development, inequalities among regions are seen as the effect of the uneven distribution of indicators such as GDP per capita, income level, employment, etc., (OECD 2003). This quantitative approach to regional development has never lost its importance within Cohesion Policy, as GDP has always been used to define the eligibility of regions to access Structural Funds, and to determine the intensity of the EU intervention (Bachtler et al. 2017).

This section outlines the changing geography of the Europe of regions as a result of the eligibility criteria adopted by Cohesion Policy, with a particular attention on the 'lagging regions' and their geographical distribution over time. Thus, its aim is not to speculate on the effectiveness of Cohesion Policy, but rather to provide a general background of the regional contexts where the planning processes being described in the special issue have taken place. The timeframe taken into consideration is the five programming cycles between 1989 and 2020, with 'less developed regions' (LDR) referring to all regions having a GDP per head of less than 75% of the Community average.

When the new Cohesion Policy began in 1989, the European Community consisted of 12 countries with vastly different demographic sizes and levels of development. For instance, the GDP per head compared to the European Community average ranged from 117% in Germany to 47% in Greece. In the initial year of the 1989–1993 period the 'less developed regions' covered the entire country of Ireland, Portugal, and Greece, including their capital cities. In Spain and Italy, the largest countries targeted by Cohesion Policy, LDRs covered a significant part of the national territory, corresponding to 58.4% and 36.7% of the domestic population, respectively. The group included some of the largest European regions – i.e. Andalusia in Spain or Campania in Italy –, which were also home to metropolitan areas and regional capitals, such as Naples (IT), Palermo (IT), Seville (ES) and Malaga (ES). After the five *Länder* of East Germany – home to around 15 million inhabitants – joined the European Community in 1990, the number of LDRs rose to 44, corresponding to around 22% of its total population.

The accession to the EU of countries, such as Austria, Finland, and Sweden in the mid-1990s brought no dramatic change to the 'geography' of Cohesion Policy in terms of the distribution of less-developed regions (see Figure 1: 1994–1999 period). In contrast, after the expansion of the European Union towards the Eastern countries was completed (2004–2007), the area with regions designated as 'less developed' nearly doubled in size. In the 2007–2013 programming cycle, the number of LDRs rose to 74, covering the whole territory of large countries, such as Poland, Romania, and Bulgaria. As a consequence of the statistical effect of this expansion (GDP in Eastern countries amounted to around 50–60% of EU average) (EUROSTAT 2010), a number of former less developed regions in countries like Sweden, Finland, Portugal, Spain, and Greece lost their previous eligibility status (see Figure 1).

It is worth mentioning, however, that there are also other reasons beyond the statistical effect of expansion to explain such changes in the eligibility status of EU regions. In the case of Ireland, for instance, during the 1990s, good performance in the expenditure of EU funds was accompanied by powerful taxation policies at national level (Barry 1999; Barry, Bradley, and Hannan 2001; Breathnach 1998). This resulted in Ireland – among the poorest countries of the EC in 1989 –, to achieve the second highest GDP per capita in Europe, as well as putting Dublin amongst the most competitive urban regions on the continent (OECD 2006). Similar processes, although of lower intensity, can be observed in other regions designated as less developed (Objective 1 regions) during the 1990s, such as the Valencia region in Spain or the Athens region in Greece (EUROSTAT 2010; OECD 2007).

In contrast, looking at the geography defined by the eligibility criteria in 2014–2020 (Figure 2), we discover that there are also regions that have never changed their 'less developed' status over a long history of planning activity. This family includes rural and low populated regions of Portugal and Greece, but also large and densely populated Italian regions, dominated by metropolitan areas, such as Naples and Palermo. Alongside the region of Porto metropolitan area (Norte), these are the only cases in which the existence of large urban agglomerations cannot be associated with changes in the 'less developed' status of their respective regions, a process that – at different times – has taken place in both national capitals (i.e. Lisbon, Athens, Bucharest) and secondary cities (i.e. Valencia ES and Thessaloniki).

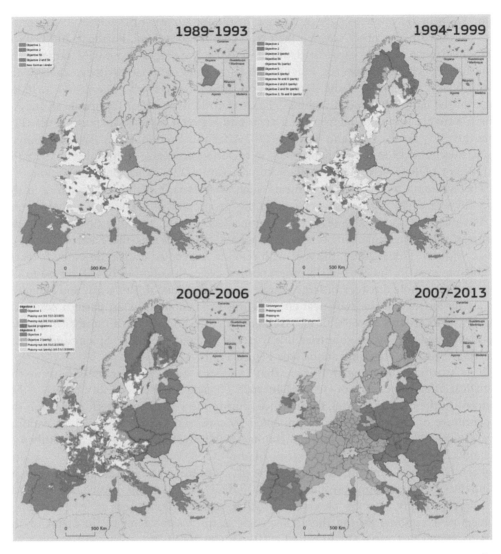

Figure 1. Geographical distribution of less-developed regions (red areas in the maps) in the four programming cycles: 1989–1993, 1994–1999, 2000–2006, 2007–2013.
Source: Author's elaboration on European Commission Official maps.

3. Dealing with regional disparities in a territorial perspective

In recent literature (Molle 2007; Barca 2009; Bachtler et al. 2017; Farole, Goga, and Ionescu-Heroiu 2018; McCann 2015; Piattoni and Polverari. 2016), it is argued that the economic performance of regions – in terms of GDP – cannot be the only key to explain the trajectories of regional development in Europe. The perspective of this paper, is that the most relevant arguments raised in that debate are: firstly, the role played by non-economic factors in the development process, as these can greatly affect regional growth and, in turn, the tendency of regions to converge; secondly, the influence of the internal structure of regions, which can be characterised by

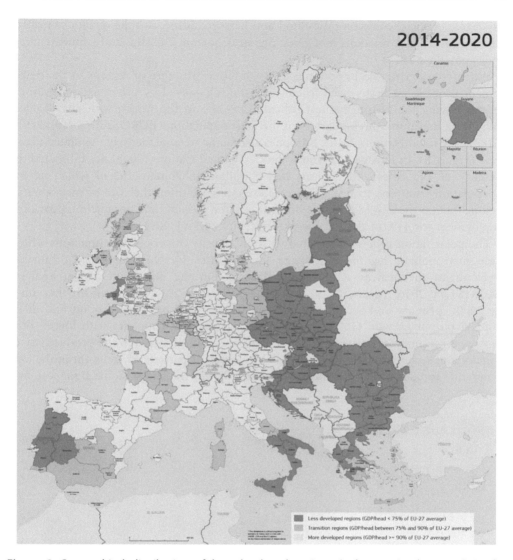

Figure 2. Geographical distribution of less developed regions (red areas in the maps) in the programming cycle 2014–2020.
Source: Author's elaboration on European Commission Official maps.

considerable development gaps between urban and rural areas, as well as between primary and secondary cities.

In relation to the first point, Molle (2007) has pointed out that divergences in regional development have to be attributed to complex interactions between the economic, social, and territorial domains in each region. Other scholars (i.e. Kutscherauer 2010) have argued that regional disparities can arise from how the 'material' resources of regions (i.e. infrastructure, environment, landscape) are connected to the 'immaterial' ones. These latter factors can include issues such as the spread of innovation capacity in both the public and private sector (Crescenzi 2011), the degree of social cohesion (Westlund and Larsson. 2016), and the quality of institutions or governance relations in a given region (Charron, Dijkstra, and Lapuente 2014; Rodríguez-Pose 2013).

When considering the importance of the internal structure of regions in the development process, we firstly need to consider the role played by urban agglomerations. Besides having the second highest urbanisation rate in the world, with city-dwellers amounting to around three-quarters of the total population (EUROSTAT 2016; OECD 2018; UN-United Nations 2018), Europe is also home to large, densely populated urban areas (Figure 3). In Europe as a whole, the UN-United Nations (2018) has estimated the presence of 146 cities with at least half a million inhabitants, 52 of which having a population from one to five million. These cities are often the core of metropolitan regions that, in the EU-28 area, are home to around 39% of total population, providing employment for 41% of the EU's workforce (EUROSTAT 2016).

The polarisation process associated with the density of people and functions within these metropolitan regions can create the premises for the emergence of further development divergences at sub-regional scale. On the one hand, recent analyses (EUROSTAT 2016; Farole, Goga, and Ionescu-Heroiu 2018) have shown that since the 2000s, primary and secondary cities in the EU have provided around half of all national output growth. On the other hand, especially in countries with low-income regions, these analyses suggest that there may be significant gaps in the productivity of primary and secondary cities (Figure 4). This process is particularly relevant in the case of national capitals of Eastern European countries (i.e. Bucharest, Sofia, Budapest, and

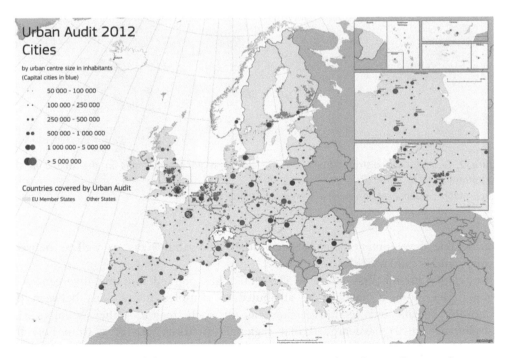

Figure 3. Population size of the European cities participating to the urban audit network.
Source: (Dijkstra and Poelman 2012).

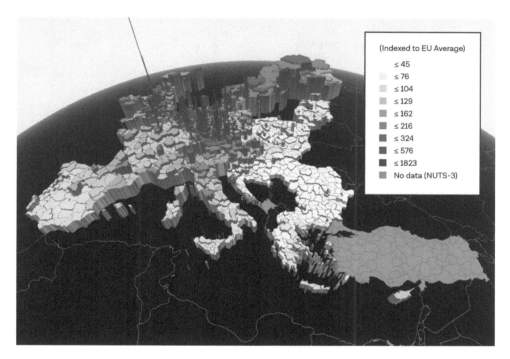

Figure 4. GDP per capita on the EU average at NUTS-3 level.
Source: Farole, Goga, and Ionescu-Heroiu (2018) from EUROSTAT data.

Warsaw), where the concentration of economic development in primary cities is often associated with increasing disparities between secondary cities and rural areas, but also between cities of similar size in countries with significant internal disparities (Figure 5).

Divergences in the urban-regional geography of Europe are, however, not new in recent history. In the eighties, when Cohesion Policy was conceived, European cities were generally depicted as places of dramatic socio-economic transformation. Many analyses emphasized the impact of post-industrial transition on urban areas, with consequences in terms of demographic decline, unemployment, social segregation, and environmental issues (Van Den Berg, Drewett, and Klaassen 1982; Cheshire and Hay 1989; Turok and Mykhnenko 2007). However, cities and regions began to be perceived as places that could be chosen to take advantage of processes, such as globalisation and European integration (Cheshire 1995; Hall 1993).

The different capacity of cities and regions to respond to these processes ended up by providing increasing diversification in the geography of urban development in Europe. In a well-known report from the French DATAR (Brunet 1989), the European territory was depicted as dominated by an 'urban core' – stretching from central England to the North of Italy – characterised by a number of networked urban regions. At the margins of this backbone, other agglomerations with 'world city' potential – i.e. Paris, Madrid, Barcelona, and Rome – were described as 'islands' surrounded by marginal regions, led by second cities or regional capitals.

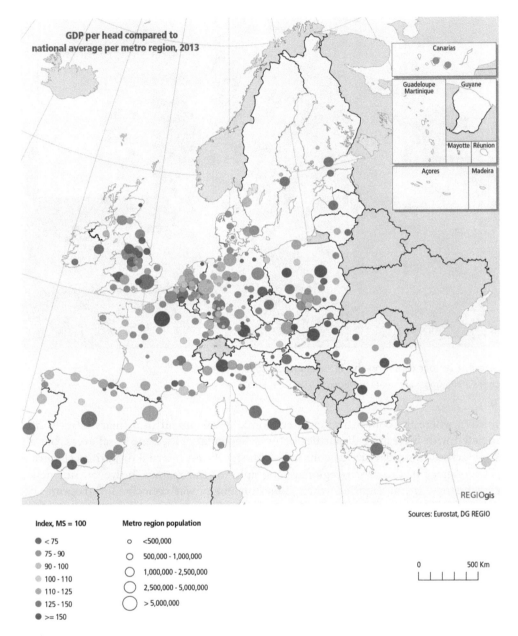

Figure 5. GDP per head compared to national average in metro regions (2013).
Source: Author's elaboration on EUROSTAT map.

A few years later, in the first comprehensive analyses of cities commissioned by the EC (Parkinson 1992), the European urban system was represented as divided into three main groups

- an 'old core', consisting of the urban areas of the first industrial revolution (covering the UK, Northern France, Belgium, the Netherlands, and Northern Germany);
- a 'new core', including the capitals of emerging/competitive regions in close proximity to the old core (covering Southern Germany, South-Eastern France, Northern Italy, and Central-Eastern Spain);
- a 'periphery' formed by primary and secondary cities of regions with problems of development, mostly placed at the geographical margins of Europe.

Marginality in that 'periphery' was explained as the result of the existence of various development gaps, often rooted in the long history of each country, including low diversification in the production system, a lack of infrastructure and transport links to the core regions, and also institutional weakness in coordinating urban policy with regional development strategies (Parkinson 1992).

While centre-periphery dualism has remained a dominant feature of other analyses on the European urban system (EC – European Commission 1994; Kunzmann and Wegener 1991; Pumain and Saint-Julien. 1996), the EU's increasing focus on the spatial implications of regional development has brought new perspectives to the role of cities in the reduction of regional disparities. For instance, the process which has led to the European Spatial Development Perspective (ECC – European Communities 1999; Faludi and Zonneweld 1997; Faludi and Waterhout 2002), by claiming for a more 'polycentric and balanced urban system' in the EU, has helped to legitimise a stronger territorial dimension within Cohesion Policy. As an outcome of that process, it is worth mentioning the inclusion of 'territorial cohesion' among the objectives of the EU, after the Lisbon Treaty was signed by member states in 2007 (Medeiros 2019).

Other more recent analytical efforts have helped to understand the links between urban and regional development across the European territory. For instance, *The State of European Cities Report* (EC – European Commission 2007) was the first document to provide a comprehensive analysis of the strengths and weaknesses of urban areas in Eastern countries after their accession to the EU, revealing their gaps in terms of prosperity and the extent of contrasts between development levels in cities and regions. These territorial issues are also well represented in the subsequent *State of European Cities Report* (EC – European Commission 2016), which provided a portrait of the European urban system since the post-2008 global crisis. In the context of increasing polarisation and subregional divergences, thanks to the availability of data at suburban level, this report has also highlighted the rise of development gaps within cities and metropolitan areas, even in the stronger EU countries (EUROSTAT 2016).

In comparative terms, these studies have also highlighted the strengthening of processes which are expected to enlarge the divergence among and within EU urban regions. Despite the crisis, in the 2010s a number of European urban areas experienced remarkable growth processes, partly in the 'old' urban core of Europe where cities are well integrated in the global networks (ESPON 2014), but also in national capitals of countries at the margins of Europe (i.e. Portugal, Romania, and Poland). As underlined before, however, this dynamism has often emerged at the expense of rural and more remote regions, accelerating their depopulation and economic decline (EUROSTAT 2016).

Another consequence of this process, equally neglected by GDP-based economic analysis, is the widening of development disparities within urban areas in growing regions, due to the existence of marginalised groups or neighbourhoods. In this regard, Barca (2009) has pointed out that inequality and social exclusion may be highly spatially concentrated, sometimes in 'pockets' close to areas with high standards of living, with the result that the 'polarisation of income inequality is not well captured by disparities in per-capita income between regions (defined at the NUTS 2 level)' (p. 33). In short, regardless of the cognitive perspective, the European urban system seems to be shaped by an increasing complexity, with different types of marginality co-existing in the same regional area.

4. Cities in the EU's regional policy

The recognition of cities as both drivers of regional development and places of development is the reason why, after the eighties, they became the target of increasing attention from the European Community. The emergence of an explicit focus on 'urban development', in particular, can be described as an incremental process characterised by various steps and different instruments, including political declarations, adjustment of funding regulations, and the implementation of programmes for cities, beginning with the 1988 regional policy reform (Williams 1996).

From the perspective of this paper, this process can be simplified into the following three main phases:

(1) the decade 1989–1999, when the political framework for the inclusion of cities within the EU regional policy was created and the first urban initiatives were promoted by the European Commission;
(2) the 2000s, during which the urban dimension was increasingly embedded within Cohesion Policy and wider responsibilities were given to regional authorities for the implementation of urban development initiatives;
(3) the 2010s, when the role of cities in regional development were reconsidered in the light of the recession and new development issues were elevated in their importance in the EU policy agenda.

(1) During the two programming cycles following the 1988 reform, cities became a recognisable object of EC regional policy due to the success of the Urban Pilot Projects (1990–1999) and the URBAN Community Initiative (1994–2006), the first programmes supported by Structural Funds directly addressed to urban areas.[4] In addition to having focused a spotlight on the development issues of European cities, these initiatives had the merit of spreading a new method of urban regeneration across the EU, based on a holistic and integrated approach to planning (Carpenter 2013).

This decade was also marked by various political actions by the European Commission, which have paved the way for a more explicit inclusion of cities among the targets of Cohesion Policy. In an initial communication to the EU Parliament (EC – European Commission 1997), it was claimed that 'urban development in future strategy building and programmes could result in an integrated strategy between actions in urban areas and in their wider regions' (p. 9) and that local authorities would have been enabled to 'participate closely in the preparation and implementation of regional development programmes' (p. 16). In a second communication, a year later (EC – European Commission 1998), the Commission emphasized the role of cities in the reduction of regional disparities, as these disparities usually 'reflect relative strengths and weaknesses of towns and cities' (p. 3), especially in the less developed areas of Europe, where local authorities were required to make a 'cultural shift towards new ways of working within the public sector and between the public, private and community sectors' (p. 6). To achieve this, it was claimed that 'integrated urban development' needed to become «an integral part of development plans, Community Support Frameworks, Single Programming Documents, Operational Programmes», and these last instruments can be explicitly referred to the 'development problems, potential and objectives for the main urban areas in the region' (p. 7).

(2) On the basis of this political background, in the 2000s attention towards urban development was further expanded in multiple directions. By ending the Urban initiative after the 2000–2006 programming cycle, the EU transferred the methods and tools for urban development to the programmes under the responsibilities of national and regional authorities (Atkinson 2015). Between 2000–2006 and 2007–2013, this led to the appearance of 'cities' or 'urban development' as thematic objectives within the Operational programmes of various EU countries (EC – European Commission 2008). As a result of EU enlargement (2004–2007) and the development problems experienced by many urban regions in Eastern countries (i.e. industrial decline, urban decay, and depopulation) (Parkinson 2006), new perspectives were taken on the urban dimension of regional development.

A stronger interaction between the urban and regional dimensions within Cohesion Policy was particularly evident in the process leading to the 2007–2013 programming cycle. For instance, the European Parliament (EP – European Parliament 2005) recommended that interventions within urban areas should be inspired by a 'spatial dialogue' between different territorial scales, enabling 'regional and local authorities and their associations to take part in negotiations and decision-making'(p. 5). The European Commission (EC – European Commission 2006) suggested elaborating coordinated strategies for those territorial scales – i.e. urban regions, metropolitan areas, networks of cities – where urban initiatives can provide a greater impact on the regional dimension, even through the creation of flexible governance settings between urban and regional authorities. Looking at the operational programmes being implemented in the 2007–2013 period, the Commission recognised that several of them – both national and regional – were built 'on the key role of cities' and that policy fields such as urban mobility and transport were designed to improve the functional 'links between the city and the region' (EC – European Commission 2009).

(3) In the last decade, optimism about the role of cities in regional development has been partly frustrated by the post-2008 economic crisis and the poor results achieved in many sectors during the 2007–2013 programming cycle (EP – European Parliament 2014; ESPON 2014; EC – European Commission 2011a, 2014). Despite this, however, cities have not lost their centrality in the EU political discourse and the debate around reforms of Cohesion Policy in the 2010s went hand-in-hand with the claim for a new 'urban agenda' (EC – European Commission 2019). The post-crisis scenario for EU urban policy is well represented in *Cities of Tomorrow* (EC – European Commission

2011b), a report prepared to outline the social, economic, and environmental challenges within urban areas in the programming period under preparation.

In order to address these challenges, the European Commission suggested reformulating some key principles of past urban policies, such as: (a) the introduction of a 'people-based' approach, with greater focus on citizens' basic needs (and less attention on area-based initiatives); (b) the promotion of new links between formal and informal governance structures at city level, giving greater importance to the third sector; and (c) a widening of the territorial targets of EU urban policy, with greater attention to urban and even metropolitan configurations.

These recommendations were embedded in the 'sustainable urban development' concept (SUD), which since 2013 (after ERDF regulation no. 1301) has been directing the key principles and tools to be adopted within cities under EU policy (EC – European Commission 2020). The main tools identified for the implementation of urban initiatives supported by the Structural Funds are: (a) the Community-led Local Development approach (CLLD), to secure a greater involvement of local stakeholders into specific territorial situations (i.e. marginal neighborhoods) and (b) Integrated Territorial Investments (ITIs), action plans under the responsibility of 'urban authorities' (i.e. municipalities, metropolitan authorities) to guarantee a thematic/spatial integration of projects within the development strategies agreed by cities (Figure 6).

It is important to underline also, that in the 2014–2020 programming period member states and regions were required to use at least 5% of the ERDF to promote sustainable urban development implementing appropriate strategies agreed with regional and local authorities. The extent of this financial investment has greatly accelerated the mainstreaming of the EU urban methods and tools into national and regional programming. In fact, in 2014–2020 more than a hundred Operational programmes across the EU (114, according to Matkó 2016) had an explicit reference to 'sustainable urban development', including countries (i.e. Belgium, Czech Republic and Italy), with national programmes focusing on large cities and metropolitan areas.

After the Pact of Amsterdam, signed in 2016 (EC – European Commission 2019, 2020), the last step of this process lies in the debate (still underway) about how to continue EU urban policy in the post-2020 Cohesion Policy.[5] Despite the expectations created by the Urban agenda agreed in Amsterdam, the regulations for 2021–2027 do not seem to have provided radical changes to the tools and mechanisms to promote sustainable urban development. The most important innovation is the return of a 'direct' programme led by the European Commission – European Urban Initiative (EUI) – expected to support cities in terms of capacity-building, in the implementation of innovative projects and the sharing of good practices across Europe (EC – European Commission 2020). In the regulation approved in 2018 (no. 372/2018), it is also stated that the share of ERDF funding devoted to addressing 'sustainable urban development' shall be increased from 5% to 6% of the total. In support of the territorialisation process, the regulations advocated further expanding the target of the urban initiatives being supported by the SFs, with the inclusion of cities of various sizes and the promotion of planning cooperation across territorial scales, from neighbourhoods to wider territories such as the Functional Urban Areas (FUAs) (EUROSTAT 2018) (see Figure 7).

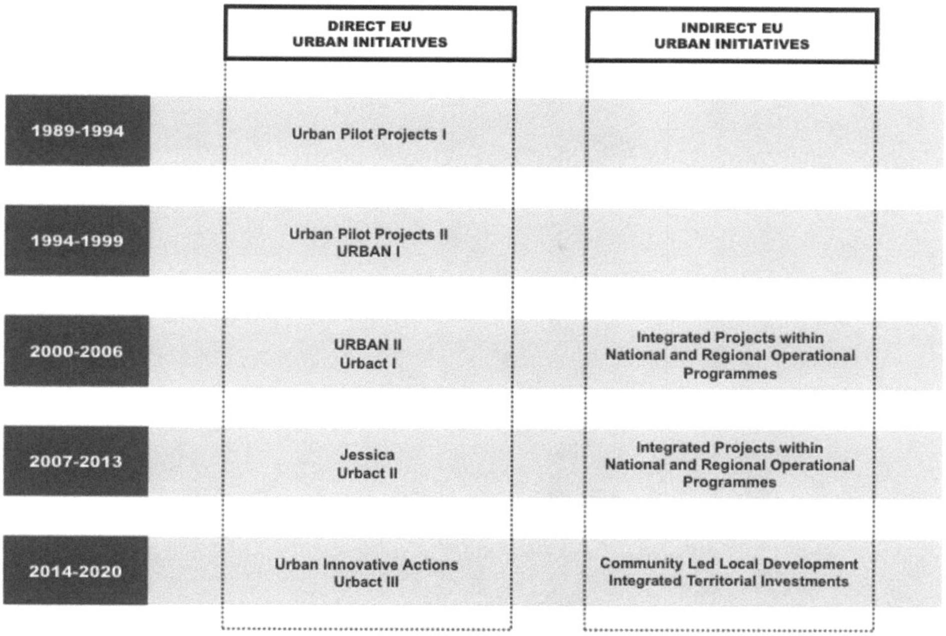

	DIRECT EU URBAN INITIATIVES	INDIRECT EU URBAN INITIATIVES
1989-1994	Urban Pilot Projects I	
1994-1999	Urban Pilot Projects II URBAN I	
2000-2006	URBAN II Urbact I	Integrated Projects within National and Regional Operational Programmes
2007-2013	Jessica Urbact II	Integrated Projects within National and Regional Operational Programmes
2014-2020	Urban Innovative Actions Urbact III	Community Led Local Development Integrated Territorial Investments

Figure 6. Main 'direct' and 'indirect' urban development instruments promoted by the EU between the 1989–1993 and 2014–2020 programming cycles.
Source: Author's elaboration.

The result of such a long process for the inclusion of urban issues among the scope of Cohesion Policy lends itself to different interpretations. For instance, some scholars have recently argued (Atkinson and Zimmermann 2016; Ramsden and Colini 2013; Tosics 2017) that we cannot look at the outcome of this process as the development of a unitary 'urban agenda' in the EU. In fact, while a number of cities have greatly benefited from Cohesion Policy over the years, the response of the EU to the overall question of sustainable urban development is characterised by both thematic and spatial discontinuity.

The first reason for such discontinuity has to be related to the changing social, economic, and environmental problems experienced by European cities over time. After the mid-1990s, when the main focus of EU interventions was still on tackling poverty and social exclusion (Atkinson 2000), increasing emphasis in policy was being given to urban competitiveness and the role of cities within the global market. Especially in the 2000s, EU institutions have largely attempted to create a balance between these two opposites, but with the result that 'what we term "European urban policy" has become trapped in the ambivalence of linking competitiveness and social cohesion' (Atkinson and Zimmermann 2016, 423). As a result, popular concepts in the EU discourse such as 'sustainable urban development' or 'place-based approach' ended up encompassing a very broad range of meanings, and various translations in terms of policy.

A second reason for policy fragmentation relates to the various social and material configurations of European cities and, consequently, the many ways action plans within EU programmes have been conceived over time in a spatial perspective. In fact, in spite

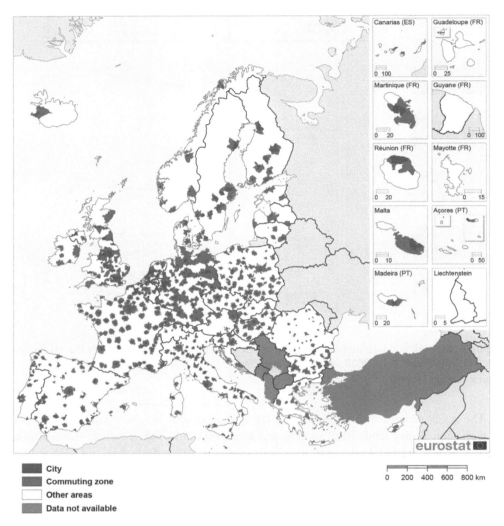

Figure 7. Functional Urban Areas in the EU (based on 2011 data).
Source: Author's elaboration on EUROSTAT map.

of the classical justification given for the inclusion of cities within Cohesion Policy – namely that around 70% of EU population live in urban areas – many have recognised (e.g. Kazepov 2005) how difficult it can be to identify a common notion of the 'European city'. Such complexity has always created problems in defining the mandate and limits of EU urban policy, as well as in understanding how sustainable urban development had to be transferred within the policy frameworks of each member state (Dossi 2017). As a result, the territorial targets of EU urban initiatives have greatly changed over time, especially since the mid-2000s, when the responsibility for the implementation of urban projects was transferred to national and regional authorities.

Just to give a few examples, until the early 2000s the target areas of EU initiatives were predominantly marginal districts in extreme socio-economic deprivation. In the

URBAN I programme (1994–1999), the target area of three-quarters of the 118 projects was a single neighborhood, with an average population of 25,000 people (GHK 2003). In the URBAN II programme (2000–2006), half of the 70 projects was located in neighbourhoods affected by industrial decline or other forms of social deprivation, with targeted areas ranging from 10,000 to 62,000 people (EC – European Commission 2010). Such spatial compactness of targeted areas was often viewed in the literature (Carpenter 2006; Chorianopoulos and Iossifides 2006) as a source of effectiveness for local action plans, since it was a precondition for funding concentration and the impact of projects.

From the 2000–2006 programming cycle onward the territorial focus of EU policy increasingly shifted from the regeneration of run-down neighbourhoods to larger urban agglomerations (Lang and Török 2017). In analyses available for the 2007–2013 period (i.e. Ramsden and Colini 2013; EC – European Commission 2008; ECORYS 2010), it is evident that Structural Funds have supported urban projects covering a wide range of territorial scales, from the neighborhood to urban and even metropolitan scales. This tendency, which clearly reflects the many faces urban issues can take across Europe, is also a response to the more holistic approach to urban policy requested within Cohesion Policy, especially after EU expansion and the Leipzig Charter approved in 2007.

When assessing the impacts of policy, many have blamed the excess of flexibility in the spatial focus of EU policy as one reason for the poor results achieved by urban interventions in many countries. Swianiewicz et al. (2011) have pointed out that good results have emerged only in countries with a strong tradition in multi-level territorial policy, including France, The Netherlands or Germany. In contrast, the lack of regional strategies or formal metropolitan authorities in many other countries (i.e. in Eastern and Southern Europe) have tended to decrease policy coordination and the impact of urban interventions at sub-regional level (Amsden and Colini 2013, Swianiewicz et al. 2011).

Despite the re-emergence of serious social issues within cities, a priority to wider urban configurations was also given in the 2014–2020 period. Deprived neighborhoods are again under the spotlight in current Cohesion Policy, but only as part of broader sustainable development strategies addressed at large cities and city-regions. Different analyses (Matkó 2016; Van Der Zwet, Miller, and Gross (2014) have highlighted that in countries, such as Italy, Romania, and Poland, the Integrated Territorial Investments (ITIs) are concentrated in metropolitan areas or networks of medium-sized cities. In other cases, however, city-region development strategies are combined with the regeneration of deprived neighborhoods, both in more developed countries (i.e. Germany and France) or in countries where less developed regions are dominated by large urban centres (i.e. Portugal and Greece) (Van Der Zwet et al. 2017).

The coexistence of different territorial scales in addressing urban development issues is still expected to play a dominant role in the near future of Cohesion Policy. In the new regulatory framework for the 2021–2027 programming cycle, support is recommended for «urban areas of any kind, acknowledging the importance of cities of various sizes and of different types of agglomerations encompassing multiple municipalities» (EC – European Commission 2020, 50). Thus, EU investments in cities should be directed at a range of territorial situations, including (a) 'urban neighbourhoods', in order to address social exclusion and the 'spatial dimension' of poverty; (b) 'cities' or 'towns', including medium-sized urban areas, where competitiveness can be more easily combined with social and environmental policy; and, not least, (c) the metropolitan scale (i.e. FUAs), where EU policy is expected to address a broad range of regional development challenges, including urban-rural linkages. More recently, the importance of these spatial dimensions to EU urban policy has been further underlined in *The New Leipzig Charter* (2020), signed by member states under the German presidency of the EU Council.

Looking at this process from a wider perspective, we must recognise that the 'urban dimension' has ended up encompassing a wide range of meanings over time (Atkinson and Zimmermann 2016), providing different keys to address the development problems and potentials of EU cities. In fact, while EU policy had to recognise the different shapes that urban issues can take within the European territory, member states have achieved increasing autonomy in applying the 'sustainable urban development' concept in their local contexts. This led to a variety of interpretations of EU policy principles and methods within the European cities, well represented in the planning histories told in the following case studies.

5. Conclusion

Given the exploratory nature of this paper, this last section summarizes a number of questions we need to consider when addressing the role of Cohesion Policy in the development process of EU cities.

In the policy process started in the late 1980s, urban development has been constantly perceived as a way to achieve regional cohesion in the European Community. Both in literature and official analyses, however, there is little evidence on the ways this process works in practice and how it can be transferred into effective policy tools. For instance, while acknowledging that EU policy has substantially influenced the development trajectories of various cities, we also need to recognise that its impact in terms of regional development and on the reduction of regional disparities is limited overall.

An explanation is that cities and regions are immersed in extraordinarily complex development processes, shaped by different driving forces (i.e. social, economic and political factors), which are only partially affected by EU policies. This is particularly relevant in many areas at the margins of Europe – in Southern and Eastern countries, for instance –, where cities are embedded in regions with serious problems of development, often inherited from peripherality in the past. In the context of these policy issues, but also of an EU strategy that is still investing on cities as engines of regional development and sustainable growth, we can limit our final considerations to the following.

(1) The link between development processes at urban and regional scale, for many reasons, cannot be taken for granted. Up until the mid-2000s, there is evidence that urban areas played a key role in boosting regional development in some European countries. In Spain, for instance, while regions had growth in terms of GDP, many regional capitals were the catalysts of change, experiencing modernisation processes that can be related to EU investments. Subsequently, similar processes can be observed in some Eastern countries (i.e. Poland), where a number of medium-sized cities have rapidly been transformed through an effective use of the Structural Funds.

The dark side of this process is that it is often accompanied by the emergence of new forms of territorial divides. Even in some countries with a polycentric territorial structure (i.e. Italy or Poland), growth in core cities has not compensated for the lack of development opportunities in rural areas, with the result that, as a whole, regions have remained characterised by various structural weaknesses. Moreover, especially since 2008, we are also witnessing a growth of disparities within urban areas, as a result of the concentration of poverty and social exclusion at the sub-urban and neighbourhood scales. This demonstrates that the polarisation processes associated with urban development can be an obstacle in the reduction of territorial disparities, which turns out to be a challenge to be addressed by future Cohesion Policy.

(2) The interaction between the urban and regional dimension in the development process, therefore, is expected to remain a key challenge in many countries and for Cohesion Policy as a whole. In a policy perspective, this challenge needs to be addressed by transferring the lessons from the positive performance of various EU planning initiatives at the urban and neighborhood level. Over the last 25 years and four programming cycles, cities were the recipients of enormous attention from EU institutions, resulting in a range of policy tools and financial opportunities. In some cases, these benefits have materialised as the (direct) result of explicit urban policies, such as the area-based initiatives under the URBAN programme, while in other cases, through the implementation of sectoral interventions (i.e. infrastructure or environmental projects) able to effect the attractiveness and sustainability of cities. Although many scholars have argued this process cannot be considered the result of a coherent 'urban agenda' from the EU, it is hard to deny that a number of cities have benefited enormously from the investments deriving from Structural Funds.

In contrast, evidence suggest that EU policies – even in the case of extremely successful area-based initiatives – have not secured broader territorial effects in terms of urban development. This issue, which has been clear to EU policymakers since the mid-2000s, has led to a growing diversification in the territorial targets of the interventions under the Structural Funds, in order to tackle the many social, economic, and environmental problems experienced in urban areas. The result of this process, however, is that the concept of 'sustainable urban development' has widened its meaning and scope and its application can vary significantly from one local context to another.

(3) Overall, the EU approach to the urban dimension in post-2020 can be read as a continuum with these recent developments. On one side, the amount of investments in cities is expected to increase, both due to 'explicit' urban policies (i.e. the European Urban Initiative, and Integrated Territorial Investments), and as a consequence of sectoral policies that can affect the health of cities, such as interventions on climate change, digital infrastructures and social inclusion. On the other side, regions and cities are being stimulated to explore the urban dimension in a broad range of territorial situations (from sub-urban to metropolitan scales), which means that local governments need to acquire the ability to read urban issues with a multi-level perspective.

While this process is expected to facilitate a stronger linkage between the urban and regional dimensions within Cohesion Policy, promoting 'sustainable urban development' is a challenge of growing complexity for both policymakers and urban scholars. In fact, the planning and implementation of EU initiatives in such a multi-level perspective are processes that can be more likely affected by political, social, and environmental factors, with greater risk for their effectiveness when these factors conflict with each other. This means, for policymakers, the search for various governance settings to support EU policy within cities and regions and, for scholars, to be aware that evaluating Cohesion Policy in urban areas can only be performed through an in-depth and context-specific research approach. That is what the authors have sought to do in the case studies in the following articles.

Notes

1. Since 1988 the eligibility of 'lagging regions' has been based on regions having an average GDP per head of less than 75% of the Community average. From 1989 to 2006 these regions were designated as 'Objective 1 Regions', while in the period 2007–2013 the term was changed to 'Convergence Regions'. Since the Regulation (EU) No 1303/2013, 'lagging regions' are designated as 'Less Developed Regions', a definition adopted both in the 2014–2020 and 2021–2027 programming cycles.
2. These principles were firstly tested within the integrated Mediterranean programmes (IMPs), an experimental initiative started in 1986 by the European Commission to assist 29 regions with problems of development in France, Italy, and Greece. IMPs inaugurated the so-called 'Cohesion policy method', consisting of the commitment for regions to prepare an explicit integrated strategy, to be implemented through the combination of a wide range of actions, to trigger endogenous and sustainable local development (Leonardi 2005).
3. A list of the official documents that have fostered the emergence of an urban dimension within Cohesion Policy can be found here: https://ec.europa.eu/regional_policy/sources/policy/themes/urban-development/agenda/urban-agenda-documents.pdf (Accessed 30 March 2021).
4. The Urban Pilot Projects, under article 10 of the ERDF Regulation, led to the implementation of 33 action plans in the period 1990–1993 and 26 action plans in the 1994–1999 period. The Urban Community Initiative was funded by the ERDF both in the 1994–1999 programming cycle, when 118 action plans were implemented, and in the 2000–2006 period, when 70 projects were supported across Europe (Carpenter 2006).
5. The EU Urban Agenda, signed on 30 June 2016 after the informal meeting of the EU Ministers responsible for urban matters, addresses 12 thematic priorities to be focused on by future urban policies. They include: jobs and skills in the local economy; urban poverty; housing; inclusion of migrants and refugees; sustainable land use; the circular economy; climate adaptation; energy transition; urban mobility; air quality; digital transition; and innovative and responsible public procurement. Two additional priorities were subsequently added: focusing on security in public spaces and cultural heritage.

Disclosure statement

No potential conflict of interest was reported by the author(s).

References

Atkinson, R. 2000. "Combating Social Exclusion in Europe: The New Urban Policy Challenge." *Urban Studies* 37 (5–6): 1037–1055. doi:10.1080/00420980050011226.

Atkinson, R. 2015. "The Urban Dimension in Cohesion Policy: Past Development and Future Perspective." *European Structural and Investment Funds Journal* 3 (1): 21–31.

Atkinson, R., and K. Zimmermann. 2016. "Cohesion Policy and Cities: An Ambivalent Relationship?" In *Handbook on Cohesion Policy in the EU*, edited by S. Piattoni and L. Polverari. 413–426. Cheltenham: Edward Elgar. doi:10.4337/9781784715670.00042.

Bachtler, J., P. Berkowitz, S. Hardy, and T. Muravska., eds. 2017. *EU Cohesion Policy*. London-New York: Routledge.

Barca, F. 2009. "An Agenda for A Reformed Cohesion Policy. A Place-based Approach to Meeting European Union Challenges and Expectations." Independent Report. Brussels: European Commission.

Barry, F. 1999. *Understanding Ireland's Economic Growth*. Basingstoke: MacMillan.

Barry, F., J. Bradley, and A. Hannan. 2001. "The Single Market, the Structural Funds and Ireland's Recent Economic Growth." *JCMS: Journal of Common Market Studies* 39 (3): 385–579. doi:10.1111/1468-5965.00302.

Breathnach, P. 1998. "Exploring the 'Celtic Tiger' Phenomenon: Causes and Consequences of Ireland's Economic Miracle." *European Urban and Regional Studies* 5 (4): 305–316. doi:10.1177/096977649800500402.

Brunazzo, M. 2016. "The History and Evolution of Cohesion Policy." In *Handbook on Cohesion Policy in the EU*, edited by S. Piattoni and L. Polverari. 17–35. Cheltenham: Edward Elgar.

Brunet, R. 1989. *Le Villes Européennes*. Paris: La Documentation Française.

Carpenter, J. 2006. "Addressing Europe's URBAN Challenges: Lessons from the EU URBAN Community Initiative." *Urban Studies* 43 (12): 2145–2162. doi:10.1080/00420980600990456.

Carpenter, J. 2013. "Sustainable Urban Regeneration within the European Union: A Case of 'Europeanization." In *The Routledge Companion to Urban Regeneration*, edited by M. E. Leary and J. McCarthy. 138–147. London-New York: Routledge.

Charron, N., L. Dijkstra, and L. Lapuente. 2014. "Regional Governance Matters: Quality of Government within European Union Member States." *Regional Studies* 48 (1): 68–90. doi:10.1080/00343404.2013.770141.

Cheshire, P. 1995. "A New Phase of Urban Development in Western Europe? the Evidence for the 1980s." *Urban Studies* 32 (7): 1045–1063. doi:10.1080/00420989550012564.

Cheshire, P., and D. G. Hay. 1989. *Urban Problems in Western Europe. An Economic Analysis*. London: Unwin Hyman.

Chorianopoulos, I., and T. Iossifides. 2006. "The Neoliberal Framework of EU Urban Policy in Action: Supporting Competitiveness and Reaping Disparities." *Local Economy: The Journal of the Local Economy Policy Unit* 21 (4): 409–422. doi:10.1080/02690940600951964.

Cotella, G. 2019. "The Urban Dimension of EU Cohesion Policy." In *The Urban Dimension*, edited by S. Medeiros, and *Territorial Cohesion*. 133–151. Verlag: Springer.

Crescenzi, R. 2011. "Theoretical Framework: A Spatial Perspective on Innovation and the Genesis of Regional Growth." In *Innovation and Regional Growth in the European Union*, edited by R. Crescenzi and A. Rodríguez-Pose. 9–29. Verlag: Springer.

Dijkstra, L., E. Garcilazo, and P. McCann. 2013. "The Economic Performance of European Cities and City Regions: Myths and Realities." *European Planning Studies* 21 (3): 334–354. doi:10.1080/09654313.2012.716245.

Dijkstra, L., and H. Poelman. 2012. "Cities in Europe. The New OECD-EC Definition." *Regional Focus* 1. Luxembourg: Office for Official Publications of the European Communities, 1–16.

Dossi, S. 2017. *Cities and the European Union. Mechanisms and Modes of Europeanisation*. London: Rowman & Littlefield International.

EC – European Commission. 1994. *Europe 2000+ Cooperation for European Territorial Development*. Luxembourg: Office for Official Publications of the European Communities.

EC – European Commission. 1997. "Towards an Urban Agenda in the European Union." Communication from the Commission to the Council and Parliament. Brussels.

EC – European Commission. 1998. "Sustainable Urban Development in the European Union: A Framework for Action." Communication from the Commission to the Council and Parliament. Brussels.

EC – European Commission. 2006. *Cohesion Policy and Cities: The Urban Contribution to Growth and Jobs in the Regions*. Brussels: Communication from the Commission to the Council and Parliament.

EC – European Commission. 2007. *State of European Cities Report*. Luxembourg: Office for Official Publications of the European Communities.

EC – European Commission. 2008. *Fostering the Urban Dimension: Analysis of the Operational Programmes Co-financed by the European Regional Development Fund (2007-2013)*. Luxembourg: Office for Official Publications of the European Communities.
EC – European Commission. 2009. *Promoting Sustainable Urban Development in Europe: Achievements and Opportunities*. Luxembourg: Office for Official Publications of the European Communities.
EC – European Commission. 2010. "Ex-Post Evaluation of Cohesion Policy Programmes 2000–06: The URBAN Community Initiative." Report. Bruxelles.
EC – European Commission. 2011a. *The Urban and Regional Dimension of Europe 2020: Seventh Progress Report on Economic, Social and Territorial Cohesion*. Luxembourg: Publications Office of the European Union.
EC – European Commission. 2011b. *Cities of Tomorrow Challenges: Visions, Ways Forward*. Luxembourg: Publications Office of the European Union.
EC – European Commission. 2016. *State of European Cities Report*. Luxembourg: Office for Official Publications of the European Communities.
EC – European Commission. 2019. *Urban Agenda for the EU*. Luxembourg: Office for Official Publications of the European Communities.
EC – European Commission. 2020. *Handbook of Sustainable Urban Development Strategies*. Luxembourg: Office for Official Publications of the European Communities.
ECC – European Communities. 1999. *European Spatial Development Perspective*. Luxembourg: Office for Official Publications of the European Communities.
ECORYS. 2010. "The Urban Dimension of the ERDF in the 2007–2013 Period: Implementation and Practice in Five European Cities". Final Report. Bruxelles.
EP – European Parliament. 2005. "Report on the Urban Dimension in the Context of Enlargement." Bruxelles.
EP – European Parliament. 2014. "The Role of Cities in Cohesion Policy." Bruxelles.
ESPON. 2014. *Territories Finding a New Momentum: Evidence for Policy Development, Growth and Investment*. Luxembourg: European Spatial Planning Observatory Network.
EUROSTAT. 2010. *Eurostat Regional Yearbook 2010*. Luxembourg: Publications Office of the European Union.
EUROSTAT. 2016. *Urban Europe. Statistics on Cities, Towns and Suburbs*. Luxembourg: Publications Office of the European Union.
EUROSTAT. 2018. *Methodological Manual on Territorial Typologies*. Luxembourg: Publications Office of the European Union.
European Commission. 2014. Investment for Jobs and Growth: Promoting Development and Good Governance in EU Regions and Cities. Sixth Report on Economic, Social and territorial cohesion. Luxembourg: Publications Office of the European Union.
Faludi, A., and B. Waterhout. 2002. *The Making of the European Spatial Development Perspective. No Masterplan*. London and New York: Routledge.
Faludi, A., and W. Zonneveld., eds. 1997. ""Shaping Europe: The European Spatial Development Perspective." Special Issue." *Built Environment* 23 (4): 257–318.
Farole, T., S. Goga, and M. Ionescu-Heroiu. 2018. *Rethinking Lagging Regions: Using Cohesion Policy to Deliver on the Potential of Europe's Regions*. Washington: World Bank.
GHK. 2003. "Ex-post Evaluation Urban Community Initiative (1994–1999)." Final Report.
Hall, P. 1993. "Forces Shaping Urban Europe." *Urban Studies* 30 (6): 883–898. doi:10.1080/00420989320080831.
Hamedinger, A., and A. Wolffhardt. 2010. *The Europeanization of Cities: Policies, Urban Change and Urban Networks*. Amsterdam: Techne Press.
Kazepov, Y., ed. 2005. *Cities of Europe. Changing Contexts, Local Arrangements, and the Challenge to Urban Cohesion*. Oxford: Blackwell.
Kunzmann, K. R., and M. Wegener. 1991. *The Pattern of Urbanisation in Western Europe 1960-1990*. Dortmund: Berichte aus dem Institut für Raumplanung.

Kutscherauer, A., ed. 2010. *Regional Disparities. Disparities in Country Regional Development: Concept, Theory, Identification and Assessment.* Ostrava: RseVŠB – Technical University of Ostrava.

Lang, T., and I. Török. 2017. "Metropolitan Region Policies in the European Union: Following National, European or Neoliberal Agendas?" *International Planning Studies* 22 (1): 1–13. doi:10.1080/13563475.2017.1310652.

Leonardi, R. 2005. *Cohesion Policy in the European Union.* Basingstoke: Palgrave Macmillan.

Matkó, M. 2016. "Sustainable Urban Development in Cohesion Policy Programmes 2014–2020, a Brief Overview". *Paper presented at Urban Development Network Meeting*, 18 February 2016, Bruxelles.

McCann, P. 2015. *The Regional and Urban Policy of the European Union.* Cheltenham: Elgar Publishing.

Medeiros, E. ed. 2019. *Territorial Cohesion. The Urban Dimension.* Verlag: Springer.

Molle, W. 2007. *European Cohesion Policy.* London-New York: Routledge.

OECD. 2003. "Geographic Concentration and Territorial Disparity in OECD Countries." Working Paper, Paris.

OECD. 2006. *Competitive Cities in the Global Economy.* Paris OECD: Publishing.

OECD. 2007. *OECD Economic Surveys: Spain 2007.* Paris OECD: Publishing.

OECD. 2018. *Regions and Cities at a Glance.* Paris: OECD Publishing.

Parkinson, M., ed. 1992. *Urbanization and the Function of Cities in the European Community.* Luxembourg: Office for Official Publications of the European Communities.

Parkinson, M. 2006. "Cohesion Policy and Cities in Europe." *Inforegio Panorama* 19: 7–10.

Piattoni, S., and L. Polverari., eds. 2016. *Handbook on Cohesion Policy in the EU.* Cheltenham: Edward Elgar.

Pumain, D., and T. Saint-Julien., eds. 1996. *Urban Networks in Europe. Réseaux Urbains En Europe.* Montrouge: INED/John Libbey.

Ramsden, P., and L. Colini. 2013. "Urban Development in the EU: 50 Projects Supported by the European Regional Development Fund during the 2007-13 Period." Final Report to the European Commission. Luxembourg: Publications Office of the European Union.

Rodríguez-Pose, A. 2013. "Do Institutions Matter for Regional Development?" *Regional Studies* 47 (7): 1034–1047. doi:10.1080/00343404.2012.748978.

Swianiewicz, P., and A. R. Baucz, A. 2011. "Background Report on the urban dimension of the Cohesion Policy post 2013". Report prepared at the request of the Polish EU Presidency, Warsaw.

Tosics, I. 2017. "Integrated Territorial Investments. A Missed Opportunity?" In *EU Cohesion Policy*, edited by J. Bachtler, P. Berkowitz, S. Hardy, and T. Muravska. 284–296. London-New York: Routledge.

Turok, I., and V. Mykhnenko. 2007. "The Trajectories of European Cities, 1960–2005." *Cities* 24 (3): 165–182. doi:10.1016/j.cities.2007.01.007.

UN-United Nations. 2018. *The World's Cities in 2018.* New York: United Nations.

Van Den Berg, L., R. Drewett, and L. H. Klaassen. 1982. *Urban Europe: A Study of Growth and Decline.* Oxford: Pergamon.

Van Der Zwet, A., J. Bachtler, M. Ferry, I. McMaster, and S. Miller. 2017. "Integrated Territorial and Urban Strategies: How are ESIF Adding Value in 2014–2020?" Final Report, Directorate-General for Regional and Urban Policy, European Commission.

Van Der Zwet, A., S. Miller, and F. Gross. 2014. "A First Stock Take: Integrated Territorial Approaches in Cohesion Policy 2014–20." *IQ-Net Thematic Paper.* 35. Glasgow: University of Strathclyde.

Westlund, H., and J. P. Larsson., eds. 2016. *Handbook of Social Capital and Regional Development.* Cheltenham: Edward Elgar.

Williams, R. H. 1996. *European Union Spatial Policy and Planning.* London: Paul Chapman Publishing.

The influence of EU policy on local policy-making, governance and urban change. Evidence from Porto, Portugal

João Igreja and Paulo Conceição

ABSTRACT
Porto has long been a site of experimentation in the field of European urban policies, implemented through different initiatives and supported by EU funding. The paper describes the different urban regeneration experiences that have been undertaken by the city, analyses the nature of the policy instruments which have been implemented, and in what ways they relate to local policy-making, governance and development. What emerges from this analysis is a more complex perspective of the relationship between local/national/European policies, which needs a broader understanding of local processes to understand the emergence and transfer of the holistic approach promoted by the EU.

1. Introduction

Since the end of the last century, urban change has increasingly gained the attention of the academic community as cities – and European cities, particularly – were experiencing tremendous social, economic and spatial transformations (Stewart 1994). At the same time, urban transformations have served to catalyse the interest of policy-makers at different levels, in their attempt to face the social and economic challenges experienced by urban areas. As a consequence, the emergence of an urban dimension in public policy has led to a diversified and at times fragmentated array of planning experiments, resulting in distinctive approaches to urban problems that can be linked, among other things, to the history, practices and cultures of each specific local context. However, other 'external' factors have contributed to the evolution of national urban policies, in particular within the European Union (EU), where the process of European integration has been actively influencing policy-making processes in various countries (Liesbet and Marks 2001; Bachtler, Mendez, and Wishlade 2013).

The EU Cohesion Policy, in particular, has enabled a range of opportunities for local change in urban policy-making, through the launching of different initiatives and the implementation of regional development programmes and financing schemes for regions and cities. The influence of these features in specific European contexts has been widely debated in the literature from various perspectives (see, among others,

Dukes 2008; Carpenter 2013; De Gregorio Hurtado 2018, 2019; Vinci 2019; Athanassiou 2020; Carpenter et al. 2020).

Portugal is among the countries that have benefited from the European Structural Funds (SFs), and whose approach to development policy, spatial planning and institutional arrangements has been strongly influenced by the EU (see, among others, Magone 2006; Oliveira and Breda-Vázquez 2012; Medeiros 2014; Campos and Ferrão 2015; Marques et al. 2018; Allegra et al. 2020). In this context, Porto emerges as one of the Portuguese cities most actively involved in the Europeanisation process, participating in EU programmes, initiatives and networks that have influenced the local policy-making process and the urban development process itself for the last 30 decades.

This article investigates how the evolution of urban policy in Portugal might be linked to the Europeanisation process, focusing on the urban regeneration initiatives developed in the city of Porto. By developing a diachronic analysis of various European and national urban policy initiatives, it seeks to explore the movement and transfer of approaches and methods gathered from the EU, whilst also attempting to understand the direct and indirect effects of these initiatives on the city's development trajectories.

The qualitative research presented in this paper is based on a mixed of official documentary sources including the analysis of legislation, planning documents, evaluation reports and institutional documents, and the review of the literature produced at both national and European levels. By tracing the possible links between policy instruments and governance changes, it seeks to contribute and better understand the following broader questions:

(1) To what extent have the EU initiatives shaped the local policy-making process, influenced local governance and stimulated an increase in planning capacity?
(2) Have the EU urban initiatives contributed to develop the city in terms of urban regeneration and local development?

The paper is structured like so: following this introduction, Section 2 presents a brief theoretical framework regarding the Europeanisation process, focusing on its implications for the transfer of urban policy methods and practices. Section 3 presents a review of the main urban-related policies that have taken place in Portugal in the last decades, with the aim of understanding how their implementation in Porto – subsequently described in Section 4 – has been affected by the EU approach. The conclusion of the paper attempts to address the research questions, highlighting the complexity of the ways in which the EU can and has affected urban policy-making and, simultaneously, how this process is hampered by local conditions.

2. The EU urban agenda and the process of policy transfer

2.1. *The urban dimension of the EU Cohesion Policy*

The building of a EU regional policy has its foundations in the Community's commitment to reduce economic disparities resulting from the process of European integration, and steer the socio-economic convergence levels between its member states (Armstrong 1995; Molle 2007). The introduction of the European Regional

Development Fund (ERDF) in 1975 and the chain of events set in motion during the 1980s by the addition of poorer Mediterranean countries and by the Single European Act (SEA), started to shape a 'genuine' EU cohesion policy (Bachtler and Mendez 2007). The Cohesion Policy itself has come a long way in terms of its objectives, contents, structure, actors and implementation mechanisms (Leonardi 2005; Piattoni and Polverari 2016). While it has been a decisive tool to reduce territorial disparities – by granting financial support – it has been fostering new policy instruments (Tofarides 2003) and governance mechanisms that seek the involvement of subnational actors in European decision-making (Hooghe 1996).

In what concerns the role that urban policy plays on regional development, the emergence of the urban dimension within the EU Cohesion Policy can be seen as the result of intergovernmental dialogue and cooperation, and a set of experimental actions associated with the Community programming cycles (see, among others, van den Berg, Braun, and van der Meer 2007; Atkinson 2015; Medina and Fedeli 2015; Cotella 2019). One of the initial landmarks of this process arose from the 1988 ERDF reforms that introduced thematic instruments to address urban issues. Consequently, throughout the 1990s, the European Commission continued to promote urban initiatives – such as the Urban Pilot Projects (UPP) or URBAN Community Initiative – and endorsed new policy tools built on the promotion of an integrated area-based approach to urban development. This was followed up with a phase of 'mainstreaming' of the urban dimension into national and regional structural programmes – with cities benefiting in a number of ways from the integration of Cohesion instruments in regional and national programmes supported by the SFs – and more recently with the introduction of the Integrated Sustainable Urban Development (ISUD) method. In the meantime, these practical experiences were accompanied by the development of knowledge regarding urban development, that in turn resulted in the publication of multiple documents and in the implementation of platforms for sharing good practices among cities (e.g. Urban Audit). All these elements have been contributing to shape the EU urban agenda.

At the same time, it is important to take into account the role and influence that the urban dimension of the EU regional policy has had over local policy-making and governance. For example, Leonardi (2005) points out that there have been visible changes related to Europeanisation occurring in the 'nature of relations between institutions' and in the emergence of 'sub-national institutions as significant actors'. It is against this backdrop that Section 2.2 describes some of the possible implications concerning the multi-level urban policy transfer of methods and practices.

2.2. *Europeanisation and urban policy change*

The process of Europeanisation and its impact on public policy is a topic widely addressed in the literature (see, among others, Börzel and Risse 2000; John 2001; Green Cowles, Caporaso, and Risse 2001; Le Galès 2002; Olsen 2002; Featherstone and Radaelli 2003; Zerbinati 2004; Antalovsky, Dangschat, and Parkinson 2005; Marshall 2005; Dukes 2008; Atkinson and Rossignolo 2010; Hamedinger and Wolffhardt 2010; Faludi 2014; Dossi 2017; Carpenter et al. 2020). As underlined by Olsen (2002), however, it is difficult to find a shared definition of this concept, and even less to find a common direction through which domestic policies are influenced by the

EU and vice versa. Among the different definitions available, Radaelli (2003, 30) suggests that Europeanisation refers to 'processes of construction, diffusion, and institutionalization of formal and informal rules, procedures, policy paradigms, styles, "ways of doing things", and shared beliefs and norms which are first defined and consolidated in the making of EU public policy and politics and then incorporated in the logic of domestic discourse, identities, political structures, and public policies'.

By referring to the necessary conditions for Europeanisation to occur, Börzel and Risse (2000) argue that a kind of 'misfit' between EU and domestic processes is required. The first variant of misfitting relates to the policy domain, which concerns local policy discourses, rules and instruments used to achieve policy goals. For instance, with reference to urban policy, one can highlight the policy orientation towards strategic planning, integrated area-based approaches, or mechanisms of civic participation. The second misfit relates to the institutional domain, which refers to procedural challenges to governance modes and institutional arrangements. In the urban policy-making process, this could be a consequence of the empowerment of specific local actors in a structured model of multi-level governance, or the involvement of private stakeholders in accordance with a partnership approach to urban regeneration.

With regard to the intensity and impact of the EU influence on domestic policies and governance structures, Börzel and Risse (2000) suggest a classification based on the following three criteria:

(1) the first, defined as 'absorption', usually happens when a Member State is 'able to incorporate European policies or ideas and readjust their institutions, respectively, without substantially modifying existing processes, policies, and institutions' (Börzel and Risse 2000, 10);
(2) the second, referred to as 'accommodation', represents a middle ground, where countries adapt 'existing processes, policies and institutions without changing their essential features and the underlying collective understandings attached to them' (ibid.);
(3) the third and final, described as 'transformation', occurs when EU countries 'replace existing policies, processes, and institutions by new, substantially different ones, or alter existing ones to the extent that their essential features and/or the underlying collective understandings are fundamentally changes' (ibid.).

The mechanisms outlined by Börzel and Risse (2000) are particular relevant to what can be considered as a 'top-down' perspective of Europeanisation, which refers to changes in policies, practices, preferences or participants within local systems of governance, arising, in the case of urban policies, from the negotiation and implementation of EU programmes. Given our assertions, however, it is also vital to make reference to the 'bottom-up' mechanisms of Europeanisation, defined elsewhere as an 'upload' process of Europeanisation (Marshall 2005).

In addition to these vertical associations, Radaelli (2003) suggests the existence of various 'horizontal' or 'soft modes' of Europeanisation, resulting from activities that stimulate a transfer of knowledge, policy learning and an exchange of experiences without the direct involvement of EU institutions. An apt example regarding European urban policies could be the different networks established by the EU (e.g.

URBACT, Eurocities) in order to disseminate urban innovation and good practices across European cities (see Atkinson and Rossignolo 2010).

Overall, there is no singular perspective to comprehensively analyse Europeanisation in the field of urban development and policy, since it is an intricate process resulting from the accumulation of different activities and relations (Marshall 2005), with the power and influence to affect the way in which actors are involved in planning activities and partnerships, the creation of networks to support projects, and how innovation is transferred both locally and across territorial levels. In that respect Atkinson and Rossignolo (2010, 204) have argued that while certain common EU-oriented ways of thinking, concepts and modes of action have been recognised to be emerging within domestic levels, the manner in which these 'are taken up and utilised by different cities will vary, often considerably, and we should not assume that the same words used in different national and local contexts have the same meaning'.

This detail reminds us that, to successfully understand the effects of EU policy discourse in local practices, we need to adopt an analytical framework capable of capturing and defining the complexity of these processes. For instance, Carpenter et al. (2020) propose an analytical framework which addresses the engagement between the EU and cities with three dimensions – direction of transfer, object of transfer, and impact of transfer –, which collectively open the way for an in-depth study of the Europeanisation of urban policies, drawing particular attention to the complex, relational and variegated nature of the process.

The complexity of processes, dimensions and directions of change, inherent in the proposals of Carpenter et al. (2020) seem nevertheless to diverge away from an understanding of the Europeanisation process as the emergence and transfer of a holistic, integrated, area-based development model, e.g. the so-called ISUD approach introduced in the context of the Acquis Urbain, fuelled by cycles of experimentation, learning and generalisation. This contrast requires, on the one hand, a more in-depth discussion and closer look at the characteristics of the intervention models that are developed. Moreover, it most certainly requires a broader understanding of the reconfiguration of urban policies.

3. Urban policies and Europeanisation process in Portugal

3.1. *From sectoral investments towards the urban dimension*

After the addition of Portugal to the European Economic Community (EEC) in 1986 and with the preparation of the SEA, a set of pragmatic policies and reforms were developed to restructure the European Community and boost its impact in national public policies (Leonardi 2006). Around the same time significant changes began to take place nationally in both spatial and urban policy systems, which had until that time remained largely undeveloped, centralised and lacked consensual strategic orientations for territorial development (Magone 2006; Domingues, Portas, and Sá Marques 2007; Oliveira and Breda-Vázquez 2011; Rosa 2018; Cavaco, Florentino, and Pagliuso 2020).

Meanwhile, in European debates increasing attention was given to cities, which became recognised as places where the problems and opportunities for regional development were concentrated. This resulted in the gradual inclusion of an urban dimension within the SFs, through the development of new instruments and guidance documents focusing on urban issues, even in respect to the autonomy of member states on this matter (van den Berg, Braun, and van der Meer 2007; Carpenter 2010; Atkinson 2015; Atkinson and Zimmermann 2016; Cotella 2019).

In consideration of the urban issues in the EC regional policy, a step forward lies in the launch of the UPP during the first European Community Support Framework (CSF, 1989–1993). This represented a significant turnaround in urban regeneration and planning policies in Portugal, and both Lisbon and Porto were among the intended cities of the programme.

During the period 1994–1999, the EC supported major national/regional infrastructural projects – e.g. motorways, basic sanitation facilities, the Alqueva dam, and a second bridge across the River Tagus –, and in contrast to the previous cycle, it included interventions with direct incidence on cities. Indeed, the European Regional Development Fund financed an Operational Programme devoted to environmental and urban regeneration with a specific sub-programme for urban renewal called Intervenção Operacional de Renovação Urbana (IORU). This instrument supported integrated measures for the regeneration of deprived neighbourhoods and the renewal of areas occupied by informal, substandard housing, as well as various projects within the framework of Lisbon's EXPO'98 waterfront project (see, among others, Ferreira and Indovina 1999).

In the same period, an even wider impact on policy-making was to take place through the implementation of the URBAN I Community Initiative. In this instance, Medeiros and van der Zwet (2019) have argued that the influence of URBAN I in Portugal cannot be limited to a tangible impact on a city's regeneration, however, it must also be evaluated in terms of an improvement of local capacities and the activation of learning processes. URBAN I has been referred to as a source of inspiration for other subsequent national programmes (e.g. Programa de Reabilitação Urbana, 1995–2004), especially in the cases that were designed to address the revitalisation of troubled urban areas (see, among others, Domingues, Portas, and Sá Marques 2007; European Commission 2011).

3.2. POLIS: physical and environmental regeneration

After the successful implementation of the URBAN I Community Initiative (see, for Carpenter 2006, 2010), the follow up programme in the 2000–2006 programming cycle is seen by many authors (Atkinson 2001, 2015; van den Berg, Braun, and van der Meer 2007; European Parliament 2014; Medina and Fedeli 2015) as a fundamental step in the consolidation of an urban agenda in the EU. In Portugal, the URBAN II programme targeted deprived neighbourhoods within the metropolitan areas of Lisbon and Porto, relied on both national and EU funding, and was supported by partnerships that integrated a wide range of stakeholders (both local and national, public and private). It has also been argued that this EU initiative had greatly influenced the creation of the Iniciativa Bairros Críticos, a pilot project launched by the national government in 2005 (Breda-Vázquez, Conceição, and Fernandes 2009; European Commission 2011).

The year 2000 marked a significant change in the Portuguese urban policy framework with the introduction of an innovative strategic programme: Programa POLIS,

2000–2006. Within the literature it has been suggested that multiple links exist between this programme and previous national and EU experiences. Some authors have pointed out that POLIS is embedded with the ideas and motivation from the EXPO'98 urban project (Domingues, Portas, and Sá Marques 2007; Rosa 2018), whilst others have underlined the analogies with the URBAN initiative, and more broadly, with the EU approach to urban regeneration (Mamede and Tavares 2010; Medeiros and van der Zwet 2019; Cavaco, Florentino, and Pagliuso 2020).

As part of a territorial development strategy aiming at strengthening the national urban system, POLIS sought to initiate an approach not based on sectoral investments and infrastructure development. As a result it acted as the catalyst for integrated spatial interventions of greater impact, that would have otherwise struggled to produce the same results (Queirós and Vale 2005). Among the operational components of the programme, the first one – integrated operations of urban and environmental rehabilitation – encouraged city councils to develop a strategic view for their cities, and subsequently to create specific partnerships between the State and municipalities in order to manage local action plans (the so-called Sociedades POLIS).

Following the 2002 change in Government, a new legislation was introduced with a direct influence in urban regeneration matters, the Decree-Law No.104/2004 of May 7th. This legal framework was a commitment to revitalise historic centres and other critical areas, and support the creation of public-private companies – Sociedades de Reabilitação Urbana, SRU – with the participation of central and local authorities. In practical terms, participating companies benefited from exclusive legal competences to facilitate administrative procedures, including the approval of building repairs, the expropriation of properties, the acquisition of the right to use public areas, and the chance to establish contracts with the private sector (see, among others, Balsas 2007; Breda-Vázquez, Conceição, and Fernandes 2009; Neto, Pinto, and Burns 2014; Branco and Alves 2020).

3.3. POLIS XXI: cities, networks of cities and integrated urban development

The importance of integrated urban development at the EU level would take a major step in the 2007–2013 period, as it was integrated into the national and regional operational programmes supported by the SFs (see, among others, Bachtler et al. 2006; European Commission 2008; Ramsden and Colini 2013). At the same time, as highlighted by Atkinson (2015, 23), cities further benefited from many Cohesion Policy instruments and initiatives, following increasing recognition that the EU 'sectoral policies have important impacts on urban areas and their development and that these policies should take into account their "spatial impact" and "urban dimension"'.

For the programming cycle of 2007–2013, the Socialist government introduced a new policy framework for Portuguese cities, called Política de Cidades POLIS XXI. While some authors have touched upon the connections to previous initiatives such as URBAN (Medeiros and van der Zwet 2019; Cavaco, Florentino, and Pagliuso 2020; Rio Fernandes et al. 2020), others have highlighted the indirect influence on POLIS XXI of policy and planning practices developed in other EU countries (see, for example, Chamusca 2011; Queirós 2014; Campos and Ferrão 2015), along with additional associations with trends arising within other sectors of EU regional policy – e.g.

promoting efficient solutions for existing facilities and/or environmental sustainability (Mourão 2019).

POLIS XXI envisaged a decentralised, bottom-up approach, able to tackle multiple territorial scopes, and make use of public/private financing sources, including allocations from the CSF. In operational terms, the policy was structured according to the following key tools: i) urban regeneration partnerships (Parcerias para a Regeneração Urbana); ii) urban networks for competitiveness (Redes Urbanas para a Competitividade e para a Inovação); and iii) innovative actions for urban development (Acções Inovadoras para o Desenvolvimento Urbano). Among these tools, the urban regeneration partnerships were of key importance in the promotion of an integrated approach to urban development in Portugal, and gained particular relevance, as evidenced by the number of projects approved and the amount of investments made across the country (European Commission 2011; Cavaco, Florentino, and Pagliuso 2020). Its main feature was the establishment of mandatory, local and flexible partnerships, led by municipalities, engaging with diverse public and private stakeholders while also strengthening citizens' participation. As pointed out by Rio Fernandes et al. (2020, 17), these were 'revolutionary participatory and governance principles' for the time, which had in fact struggled to be assimilated into the processes of urban areas strategic planning and management.

Running parallel to these developments, additional aspects were introduced into the national urban policy framework in 2009. On the one hand, the establishment of a new legal scheme for urban regeneration (Decree-Law DL No.307/2009 of October 23rd) established with more accuracy the role and scope of urban regeneration companies (SRU), along with the consolidation of rehabilitation fiscal incentives. The document reinforced the national spatial planning instruments by introducing an urban regeneration normative framework at both programmatic, procedural and executive levels. In addition it established a company's role within the wider spatial planning tools (Neto, Pinto, and Burns 2014). On the other hand, the creation of the JESSICA Holding Fund Portugal counteracted the impacts of the financial crisis and facilitate the implementation of the community initiative in the national territory. In turn, the fund has helped the rehabilitation of degraded buildings with private capital, by using European grant funding to make repayable investments in the form of equity, loans or guarantees.

3.4. *Cidades Sustentáveis 2020: instrumental alignment to the EU integrated sustainable urban development*

Due to the economically adverse post-crisis scenario, it was crucial for Portugal to make the best use of EU funding. Thus, while the 2014–2020 programming cycle was under development, the country had the opportunity to capitalise on former urban policy experiences, and develop an improved, coherent and sustainable urban development policy framework. In broad terms, the country's commitment to embrace these new challenges was demonstrated through the following two elements:

(1) a new strategic framework for cities – Cidades Sustentáveis 2020; and
(2) a partnership agreement with the EC – Portugal 2020.

The first, approved in 2015 by the central government, outlined the principles and guidelines for sustainable spatial and urban development and its main goal was to promote the functional, cultural, social and economic development of urban areas. The strategy was 'built on an integrated action framework, demanding for the coordination between the several government levels, the integration of a wide range of policy sectors and citizens' participation' (Cavaco, Florentino, and Pagliuso 2020, 59). However, one important aspect that should be underlined relates to the lack of operational capacity. Unfortunately, the framework didn't encompass direct links to financing or implementation, which would be framed within Portugal 2020.

The Portugal 2020 framework introduced new approaches for territorial sustainable development and, in its efforts to create sub-regional development strategies, gave additional responsibility to inter-municipal institutions. Specifically, the Integrated Urban Development Actions were designed to promote urban regeneration and revitalisation in urban centres, based on strategic plans – Planos Estratégicos de Desenvolvimento Urbano – to be prepared by municipalities. These plans were, in a certain way, similar to the ones developed under POLIS XXI partnerships (Rosa 2018; Medeiros and Van Der Zwet 2019; Rio Fernandes et al. 2020), and local authorities were requested to develop them in order to be granted EU funding. In addition, they contained a series of sub-strategic tools:

(1) Sustainable Mobility Plan (Plano de Mobilidade Urban Sustentável, PMUS);
(2) Urban Regeneration Action Plan (Plano de Ação para a Regeneração Urbana, PARU); and
(3) Integrated Action Plan for Deprived Communities (Plano de Ação Integrado para as Comunidades Desfavorecidas, PAICD).

The practical application of this framework is yet to be thoroughly and comprehensively analysed. As mentioned by Rosa (2018) the implementation of this 'complex and fragmented' framework led in some cases to spatial, temporal and institutional overlays between the different tools. Furthermore, Cavaco, Florentino, and Pagliuso (2020, 69) argue that it resulted in 'the pulverization of funds through a myriad of tools, demanding for strategic documents and action plans, whose coherence and intelligibility are, at best, hard to scrutinize and understand'.

Similarly to other southern European countries, the need to reconcile the Portuguese urban system with the innovative framework from the EU, proved to be a demanding task (Tosics 2016). This was locally emphasised by the 'lack of articulation between this type of strategic documents and the statutory planning tools in force' – e.g. Municipal Director Plan (Plano Director Municipal) (Cavaco, Florentino, and Pagliuso 2020, 62). Moreover, Medeiros and van der Zwet (2019, 16) stressed that in order to increase the impacts on the quality of life it would have been more appropriate to link these instruments with other urban development funding initiatives, and despite the presence of 'placed-based and long term strategies mobilized by local and regional stakeholders' the expected impacts in relation to the actual needs of the targeted areas were 'somewhat limited' in comparison to the previous initiatives.

Figure 1. Location of Porto, the Metropolitan Area of Porto and Portugal in the EU-27. Source: authors.

4. The case of Porto

Porto gives name to the largest urban conurbation in the north of Portugal – Metropolitan Area of Porto – which in 2011 represented approximately 17% of the country's total population dispersed across seventeen municipalities (see Figure 1). According to the 2011 census the city's population was 237,591 and projections for 2019 estimated it would fall to 216,606. Between 1991 and 2011, the population growth rate in both Portugal and the two metropolitan areas had been positive, in contrast to the country's two main cities (Lisbon and Porto). Seixas (2008) points out that Porto's trajectory was particularly linked with the intense development of housing programmes on the peripheries of the city. In the 1970s, this process intensified with housing cooperatives focusing on neighbouring municipalities. Sousa and Pinho (2016) offer two additional reasons for the general population decrease in the city. On the one hand, the general deindustrialisation process and shift towards the tertiary sector, and on the other changes in living standards that led people to move away.

With the addition of Portugal to the EEC in 1986), steady improvements were carried out on the transport network at the metropolitan level, along with an easier access to mortgage loans for housing construction or purchases (Rio Fernandes 2011). In contrast, the troubling condition of Porto's historic city centre didn't help the situation, and as suggested by Costa (2011), strongly contributed to the shrinking phenomenon in the municipality. The subsequent revitalisation strategies have attempted to counteract this situation, but the pursuit for new residential areas offering more affordable housing has been stronger, and a younger, more active and willingly mobile population has been moving away from the city (Oliveira, Martins, and Cruz 2013).

As centre of the metropolitan area and Norte region, Porto provides the main services and acts as the socio-economic engine of Northern Portugal, standing out as an attractive historic and cultural hub. The city has been a front-runner in taking advantage of EU Structural Funds, through the implementation of different initiatives, projects and networks that date back to the early 1990s. The intersection of these experiences with various national/local planning initiatives has fostered significant changes in the city structure and organisation, whose effects will be explored in the Section 4.1 through a diachronic description.

4.1. *Prior to EEC membership: the role of the CRUARB*

Although this paper is focused primarily on the period beginning with Portugal's induction into the EEC, it is important to clarify some characteristics of the preceding periods, particularly those related to the perception of Porto's urban problems as well as the methodologies and organisation of public interventions.

During the period under the authoritarian regime of 'Estado Novo', two problematic situations arose. On the one hand, the sanitary and housing problems associated with the so-called 'islands' ('ilhas'), urban spaces of substandard housing, situated in various parts of the city, the inner part of built plots, developed throughout the earlier period of industrialisation. This situation motivated, in the 1950s, the intervention plan by the municipality (Plano de Melhoramentos), based on the construction of social housing estates in the more peripheral areas of the city, aiming to relocate some of the population from the 'ilhas'.

On the other hand, the recognition of the problems concentrated in the historic city centre in the late 1960s stimulated a debate between two opposing perspectives of intervention: one based on the idea of urban renewal, with greater focus on physical interventions, and the other that can be associated with a (contemporary) concept of integrated urban regeneration, based on an important methodological study carried out by architect Fernando Távora. According to Pinho (2009, 805), the Study for Ribeira-Barredo Urban Renewal, 'is the first Portuguese initiative aimed at promoting a true urban rehabilitation policy' (author's translation) and has influenced many other experiences in Portugal, namely on the rehabilitation of historic centres.

Following the democratic revolution, these two problems – and the social movements that arose around them – gave rise to two experiments, promoted by central administration. In 1974 the ruling transitional government created a special purpose organisation – Comissariado para a Renovação Urbana da Área Ribeira-Barredo, CRUARB – which would be responsible for developing alternatives for the critical areas of the historic centre, anchored in social and housing interventions that aimed to provide better living conditions and the restoration of historical, cultural and built heritage (Queirós 2013). Its model of intervention focused initially on housing conditions, and was based on a process of acquisition (including compulsory purchase), rehabilitation and distribution of housing by the CRUARB. Meanwhile, a short-term experiment was developed (Serviço de Apoio Ambulatório Local), to counteract the housing issues and the particular problem of the 'ilhas' by carrying out physical interventions and participatory processes to involve organised groups of residents (see Bandeirinha 2007).

In 1982, the central administration transferred its CRUARB responsibilities to the municipality. This led to the CRUARB extending its intervention area, a decrease in its investment capacity and, for several actors, a loss of influence (Lobato and Alves 2012) or a step backwards in relation to urban policies in the city centre (Queirós 2007).

4.2. A more integrated area-based approach: the role of poverty III, UPP and URBAN

As mentioned in Section 4.1, after Portugal's induction into the EEC, urban policies in Porto were marked by two complementary developments. On the one hand, a strategy of active participation in community initiatives and programmes such as Poverty III, UPP, and later on, URBAN. Whilst on the other hand, a set of investments directed mainly to enhance infrastructure, in the light of a strategic move to empower the role of the city as core of the Metropolitan Area of Porto.

It is in this context that new partnership structures were created. In 1990, an agency was created to manage different EU funding opportunities (Fundação para o Desenvolvimento da Zona Histórica do Porto, FDZHP), due to the fact that the municipality couldn't negotiate directly with the EU. The FDZHP overlapped in part with the target area of the CRUARB but focused primarily on social care activities to fight poverty and the segregation of underprivileged social groups. At the same time, it was able to combine non-material initiatives with physical interventions and promote cooperation among community actors. The complementarity of the FDZHP and the CRUARB may be seen as an important area-based initiative in the city centre, since it mirrored a local level network approach that encouraged institutional cooperation, created space for interaction and assisted with the production and sharing of knowledge (Rio Fernandes 2011; Lobato and Alves 2012).

Due to its involvement in the UNESCO World Heritage Site project and proximity to the historic centre, from 1994 to 1998 the CRUARB was responsible for the implementation of the Urban Pilot Project in Porto. The target area of the project was one of the most deprived neighbourhoods in the historic city centre (UPP Bairro da Sé, see Figure 2). Its principal objective was to provide the appropriate development conditions in an area with high levels of physical and social degradation, yet which also possessed great potential in terms of heritage and cultural richness. Considered by some

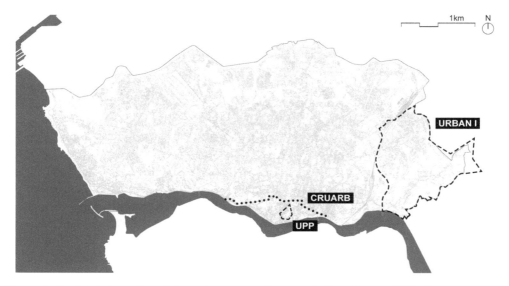

Figure 2. Spatial delimitation of the main urban policy tools in Porto in the 1990s. Source: authors.

to be the first integrated operation after about 20 years of urban interventions in Porto (see Câmara Municipal do Porto 1998), the UPP was seen as highly innovative at both city, regional and national levels. The innovations were reflected in the participation of a wide range of partners (including private stakeholders and central/local institutions), in the creation of a multidisciplinary local management team responsible for the implementation of carefully planned objectives, and an integrated approach combining socio-economic, environmental and cultural objectives.

In 1994, the city council expanded the critical area in need of recovery and the CRUARB became the leading actor responsible for the development of urban regeneration processes of the city (see also Figure 2). Two years later the historic city centre was classified as a UNESCO World Heritage Site and the CRUARB played a key role in the application proceedings (Balsas 2007). During the second CSF (1994–1999) the recently introduced sub-programme IORU channelled substantial financial allocations to support integrated measures to deal with the renewal of areas occupied by shanties homes and the regeneration of impoverished zones. Whilst in Lisbon it supported the EXPO'98 integrated waterfront renewal project, in Porto it was strongly linked with national rehousing policies by providing public facilities within social housing estates located on the periphery of the city.

In this period, Porto was among the cities selected for the URBAN I Community Initiative and its action was combined with ongoing (non-systematic) interventions. The target area (see Figure 2) was mostly residential – including several social housing blocks that were the result of different past re-housing initiatives –, which had over time faced several challenging situations due to poor urban planning, the presence of illegal constructions, or a lack of social facilities. Nonetheless, the programme sought to take advantage of a good tradition of associative life and neighbourly relations in the area which made the initiative much easier. The social dimension of urban regeneration was the programme's top priority, and the following principles guided its implementation: i) participation; ii) partnership; and iii) self-evaluation (FDVC 2001).

A decisive factor in the effectiveness of the project was the integrated approach managed by a partnership structure created for this specific purpose: Fundação para o Desenvolvimento do Vale de Campanhã.[1] This agency included local authority representatives from different areas which was vital in order to garner political support at a higher level. In contrast to the UPP, where the ongoing urban regeneration project was adapted to accommodate the 'EU model of integrated development', URBAN I tried to establish a more radical transformation of existing practices in local policy-making (European Commission 2003).

Narrowing our scope of view to the involvement of stakeholders there were contradictory interpretations regarding the extent of the public participation process. On the one side, Guerra (2004) argued that the participation quality was not truly a real integrated strategy, and the ex-post evaluation (see European Commission 2003) reported little support and cooperation from the private sector. But opposed to this, Alves (2008) pointed out that participation procedures were well planned and realised, resulting in a change of culture that affected the implementation of other initiatives which followed.

4.3. *The role of investment in public space, culture and heritage, and the rise of a more entrepreneurial model of intervention*

With the turn of the century, Porto faced many changes in terms of the institutional organisations, political agendas and spatial strategies. In 2000, the main national urban policy initiative (Programa POLIS) sought the improvement of living standards in cities through integrated operations of urban regeneration and environmental enhancement. To achieve such objectives, it used EU funding and promoted work in partnership. Porto took advantage of the already existing Porto2001 company, and combined various funding sources to carry out different interventions in the city. These actions not only met POLIS goals, but also contributed to the urban regeneration actions related to the European Capital of Culture framework.

POLIS was implemented through two waterfront interventions (see Figure 3): i) an integrated operation of urban and environmental regeneration in the west part of the city; and ii) an intervention in the historic Ribeira waterfront. These actions brought previously overlooked spaces back to life, and it was possible to note some complementarity through the interventions undertaken by the neighbouring municipalities under the same programme. However, and despite the national commitment to develop integrated spatial interventions at city level, some authors argue that it failed to achieve such orientation, and, ultimately, the interventions were mainly physical (see Breda-Vázquez and Alves 2004).

With the aim of providing the best possible conditions for hosting the European Capital of Culture events, Porto2001 assumed the exclusive responsibility of promoting cultural activities and an urban revitalisation programme for the city centre. The objectives of Porto2001 included the recovery of public spaces, the re-adaptation of key cultural and public facilities, an independent programme for the modernisation of commerce, housing refurbishment strategies, and actions linked to mobility (Balsas

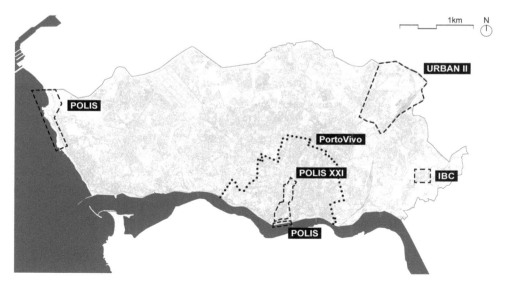

Figure 3. Spatial delimitation of the main urban policy tools in Porto between 2000 and 2014. Source: authors.

2007; Queirós 2007; Câmara Municipal do Porto and PortoVivo 2010). Despite its strategic intention to integrate a wide range of dimensions and a significant financial investment, many have highlighted the large gap that existed between strategy and implementation – the expectations for the city and what was actually done. In particular, Balsas (2004) pointed out that activities were too dispersed and extensive for the implementation timeframe, and the governance model struggled to foster good and transparent communication among stakeholders. Nevertheless, the event managed to induce transformation within specific areas of the city, which were followed by particularly large investments in a light railway system looking to favour the accessibility towards the centre of the city (Rio Fernandes 2011).

After the 2001 municipal election, the newly elected mayor's political agenda featured the introduction of a different urban regeneration strategy, paying greater attention to the entire city centre and not just the UNESCO historic area (Queirós 2007). The institutions responsible for acting specifically in the historic centre (CRUARB and FDZHP) were dissolved, and under a new political discourse emphasis was placed on 'the idea that public funding would never be sufficient to solve all problems, and private investment was thus essential' (Rio Fernandes 2011, 295). Lobato and Alves (2012) argued that this strategy can be read as a replacement for the social character of previous measures with the introduction of new market-based and efficiency-oriented ideas.

Accordingly, in line with the new emerging style in local politics, a partnership was created between the State and the municipality (PortoVivo) with the aim to operate with more freedom in the implementation of urban development strategies and programmes (Alves and Branco 2018). In 2005, PortoVivo laid out its urban and social renewal project for the city centre that reflected, in the words of Queirós (2007), a new stage of urban planning characterised by the desire to place Porto in the competitive scenario of the European urban system. The partnership focused its more immediate attention towards priority areas for intervention that included the historic centre and Baixa district (Zona de Intervenção Prioritária, see also Figure 3).

In a study concerning the impact of PortoVivo (see Neto, Pinto, and Burns 2014), some interesting points were raised by different stakeholders involved in the urban regeneration activities. On the one hand, the efficiency of the company carrying out building recoveries was complementary. But, on the other, the overall struggles they encountered when dealing with social matters, and the difficulty in improving the public realm didn't work in their favour. However, there did seem to be a shared feeling that the city centre had become much livelier after the creation of PortoVivo, although many recognise that revitalisation might have had their origins outside or before the company's interventions. Finally, some urban regeneration agents expressed the feeling that if PortoVivo had never existed, the situation would have aggravated, as the company played an important role in the medium term transformations, making the best out of the external opportunities, and therefore reducing the impacts of external threats (Sequeira 2011; Branco and Alves 2018).

In the period 2000–2006, with the launch of the URBAN II initiative, Porto took the opportunity to tackle the persisting issues rooted in the neighbourhoods close to the URBAN I target area (see Figures 2 and 3). The URBAN II project was a result of a joint application with the neighbouring municipality Gondomar, and its management was assigned to a regional body. The intervention covered critical areas from both municipalities which consisted of a large number of social housing blocks created during the rehousing initiatives (see Figure 3). The European Commission (2010) later underlined the positive performance of the programme, based on a balanced integration of physical, social and educational measures and was apparently supported by a strong participation of non-institutional stakeholders. In contrast, in the scholarly literature (see Alves 2013, 2017) it is argued that the decision-making processes revealed a strong, sectoral and top-down approach, along with the creation of weak forms of institutional collaboration between the local authority and local associations Furthermore, Alves has also pointed out that the experience with the URBAN II project was an isolated one, as the central and local administrations missed the opportunity to take advantage of the synergies that had been fostered and paid little attention to mainstreaming the planning activities that had been previously implemented.

In the framework of the pilot project Iniciativa Bairros Críticos, 2005 saw the launch of an operation to support the regeneration of Lagarteiro, a deprived neighbourhood in the east part of the city (see Figure 3) (Breda-Vázquez, Conceição, and Fernandes 2009). According to Costa (2015)the initiative worked much better than previous URBAN projects due a narrower spatial focus of the action and a stronger governance structure, with public and private partners involved at all different levels. However, some coordination issues were identified, namely between central and local administration which hindered the operation's implementation.

Recognising the persistence of social and physical degradation patterns in the historic centre, in 2005, PortoVivo developed a new urban rehabilitation strategy for Morro da Sé. It introduced a new vision for the neighbourhood, based on the development of cultural, commercial, touristic and leisure activities, and housing. The strategy was subsequently implemented through two programmes: i) an action programme funded by POLIS XXI, and ii) a resettlement programme financed by the European Investment Bank. Furthermore, under POLIS XXI the municipality and PortoVivo established different local partnerships that were intended to boost the participatory models of governance between citizens, urban stakeholders and public administration. Although the strategy recognised the need for a multidimensional approach – in which social, economic, cultural and environmental assets were taken into consideration –, physical regeneration prevailed over social measures (Rio Fernandes 2011; Mourão 2019). In total, three action programmes were implemented (Morro da Sé, Mouzinho/Flores, and Avenida), benefiting not only from European funding, but also from private stakeholders funds (see Figure 3).

Finally, in 2009, a new legal instrument was adopted to promote urban regeneration: Decree-Law No.307/2009 of October 23rd. This introduced a new normative framework that emphasised the role of the urban regeneration companies (SRU) and stressed the financial complementarity between public investment and the landowner's duty to carry out rehabilitations, as well as the need of public participation during planning stages (see, among others, Neto, Pinto, and Burns 2014). In the case of Porto that role was given to PortoVivo, which as a consequence expanded its area of interest.

4.4. Porto and the new urban agenda for the EU

During the 2014–2020 programming cycle new tools were introduced as an attempt to 'formalise' the EU-National urban agenda (see Section 3.4). Portugal embraced these new instruments through the partnership agreement with the EC: Portugal 2020. This framework sought differentiated strategies for territorial development, and mirrored the specific characteristics of each regional context. Therefore, Porto, as part of North region, was involved in the development of a complex set of strategic plans in order to maximise its accessibility to EU funding.

Among them, the mandatory urban development plan to access European financing – Plano Estratégico de Desenvolvimento Urbano – was designed by the municipality in agreement with the national spatial planning framework to encourage urban development. Two actions plans, strongly related to urban regeneration were embedded in the documentation, accounting for a planned investment of more than 200 million euros (Câmara Municipal do Porto 2015). The first recognised the necessity to consolidate ongoing processes of urban regeneration – Plano de Ação de Regeneração Urbana (PARU) –, and was subdivided in three territorial typologies in accordance to the particular strategies that were to be implemented (see Figure 4, PARU numbered accordingly):

(1) Historic waterfront (frente ribeirinha da cidade histórica);
(2) City centre (eixo central da cidade histórica); and
(3) Old industrial area (envolvente do antigo matadouro e praça da Corujeira).

The documentation established a group of measures that would benefit from public and private investment (Câmara Municipal do Porto 2015): i) the requalification of public spaces; ii) the enhancement of the ecological urban structures; iii) the rehabilitation of

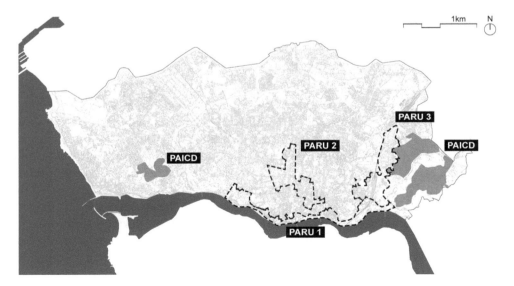

Figure 4. Spatial delimitation of the main urban policy tools in Porto since 2014 (PARU numbers according to the order in the text). Source: authors.

public facilities; iv) the reconversion of old industrial spaces; and v) rehabilitation of the housing stock. Regarding housing in the context of urban regeneration, the strategy encourages private interventions and for that matter several financial instruments have been launched by the central state, that support interventions in construction by capitalising on new housing regulations, and seeking to attract private dynamics.

The second one – Plano de Ação Integrado para as Comunidades Desfavorecidas (PAICD) –, focused on issues related to deprived communities and in this context, the municipality identified three areas where socio-economic and environmental issues persisted (see Figure 4). These areas were mainly characterised by the presence of social housing and 'ilhas', places with a high rate of unemployment and people at risk of poverty and social exclusion. PAICD was a clear expression of the integrated approach promoted by the EU during the period 2014–2020, combining small physical interventions with welfare projects focused on action groups to fight social exclusion and poverty under the community-led local development instruments.

In terms of the urban regeneration actors, PortoVivo – a former partnership between the municipality and central administration – became fully owned by the municipality in 2017. This meant a spatial expansion of the area under the SRU's responsibility, as well as a redesigning of its mission, which ended up including interventions in the affordable housing.

Finally, other municipally owned companies have been acting with direct and indirect influence on the city's urban regeneration. In particular, DomusSocial is a municipal housing company which is currently linked to interventions in social housing neighbourhoods – including the maintenance of built stock, social facilities and the development of social projects –, and also inherits the responsibility for managing assets in city's historic centre previously owned by the FDZHP.

5. Conclusion

The Europeanisation process of Portuguese public policies has been widely discussed at different levels. Several authors recognise the centrality of the 'Europe effect' in explaining the changes that occurred in Portugal in the fields of urban policies (Cavaco, Florentino, and Pagliuso 2020), of spatial planning (Campos and Ferrão 2015) and, more indirectly, of housing policies (Allegra et al. 2020). In Section 3, in particular, illustrates the emergence of a more explicit urban policy in Portugal, in contrast to the previous situation characterised by greater fragmentation and a lack of attention to city development (Parkinson et al. 1992; Domingues, Portas, and Sá Marques 2007).

Similarly to other European countries with a hierarchical and centralist tradition (Dukes 2008; De Gregorio Hurtado 2019; Carpenter et al. 2020), Portugal has shown to be keen on the processes of Europeanisation and there seems to be an understanding that in Portugal the EU has influenced domestic changes to various degrees and directions. Indeed, in addition to financial opportunities that have enabled the development of projects that otherwise would have not been achieved, European funding acted as a source of institutional change (Oliveira and Breda-Vázquez 2011, 2012; Oliveira, Ferreira, and Dias 2019), and stimulated the introduction and consolidation of urban policies and spatial planning tools (Magone 2006; Medeiros 2014; Allegra et al. 2020; Cavaco, Florentino, and Pagliuso 2020).

In this context, this paper underlines the relevance of this process in Porto, a city where implementation of different EU initiatives and programmes (for example, Poverty III, UPP, URBAN I and II, URBACT) has led to, and is the result of, a continuous tension towards the opportunities made available by the EU. There are many studies that analyse the innovations associated with these experiences (Gros 1993; Rio Fernandes 2011; Alves 2013), leading to different forms of policy transfer and related to innovations in both planning instruments and approaches to governance. However, by analysing the sequence of policy instruments and institutional configurations that characterise the case of Porto, we cannot conclude that policy transfer has followed a linear process over time and, even less so that a single model of intervention has been preferred to others.

It can be argued that the case of Porto is, above all, indicative of the diversity and tensions that characterise urban policies. In this context, governance practices and institutional design are a central aspect for understanding the processes of continuity and change in urban regeneration practices. Some tensions can be related to scale, both the scale that can define the problems and the scale on which the solutions are based. In the Porto case, at each moment, 'area-based' interventions coexist with more general interventions at the scale of the city or at the metropolitan scale. Moreover, even within an area-based concept, urban regeneration practices in the city centre have taken different trajectories than those on the more peripheral areas of the city. Overall, it should be noted that the recent transformations of urban policies in Portugal reveal the growing importance of different scales – from the city to the inter-municipal levels.

The period under observation in this paper is particularly intense in terms of institutional creation and governance transformation. Three aspects can be underlined in this respect. Firstly, the diversity of organisational settings through which municipal action is developed across the planning periods. Secondly, the changes operated in the partnership structures, between the intervention of the central administration and the intervention of the local administration. And thirdly, the persistent adaptation of the scope and territoriality of these different organisations. As a result of these processes, evidence suggests that the implementation of EU projects in Porto has not followed a single intervention model, but can instead be read as the expression of different perspectives of the city's development, as well as the of various approaches utilised for public intervention to stimulate urban development.

The CRUARB's initial experience underlies the central role of the State in housing rehabilitation. Subsequently, the role of public investment in public spaces and cultural facilities was seen as an essential trigger for urban change. PortoVivo represents a more entrepreneurial model directed to attract and facilitate private investment in the central part of the city. This diversity can be explained by the evolution of the local urban context, but it is also clearly marked by processes of political change in the management of the city, and reveals important tensions constantly present and active in its urban regeneration project. At the same time, it serves to reveal a number of continuities, as for example, the link that can be established between the CRUARB's UPP and the later experience of PortoVivo in Morro da Sé.

Taking into proper consideration the difficulty to 'isolate' the effect of EU policies, we can argue that European projects have triggered, in different modes, urban change in Porto. By referring to Portugal as a whole, Medeiros and van der Zwet (2019, 16) argued that EU funding 'positively contributed to improving physical and socio-economic elements in several deprived urban neighbourhoods (but) had limited impact in terms of changing socio-economic paradigms in urban areas which are strongly affected by drug-addiction, lack of economic capacity, and low-income levels'.

In Porto, the target areas of almost all urban regeneration programmes witnessed an intervention continuity over time (compare Figures 2, 3 and 4) which is often seen as a source for their effectiveness. As a result, the connection observed between the UPP, URBAN I and II projects have, to some extent, provided improvements in the quality of the built environment, and reduced of socio-economic marginality in both the city centre and peripheral areas (Câmara Municipal do Porto 1998; FDVC 2001; ECOTEC 2010; Rio Fernandes 2011). In the old town, particularly, EU interventions clearly contributed to the recovery of historic buildings and monuments, the creation of pedestrianised zones and public spaces, and the upgrading of public facilities.

The role played by EU programmes in the revitalisation of the city over the last 30 years, however, should be also observed through the lens of other political, institutional and social processes. For instance, the neo-liberal turn of urban policy in the last 15 years (Queirós 2007; Sequeira 2011; Alves and Branco 2018) is a powerful argument in explaining the increase of gentrification or the 'floating city users' phenomenon in different neighbourhoods (Carvalho et al. 2019; Santos and Branco-Teixeira 2020).

In conclusion, the raising alignment of the Portuguese urban policy brought up to speed with international and EU strategies and tools, contributed to enlarge and strengthen the scope of national urban policy (Cavaco, Florentino, and Pagliuso 2020) introducing changes that might be seen as the direct result of the Europeanisation process. In the case of Porto, however, complex relationships have emerged between local, national and European urban policies, resulting from a long sequence of new governance models, institutional re-organisation, and policy-making practices.

Note

1. The Fundação para o Desenvolvimento do Vale de Campanhã was created in 1995 for the purpose of managing the URBAN I that targeted the specific Vale de Campahã area. Without changing its initial purpose of tackling social issues of the city, it was renamed Fundação para o Desenvolvimento Social do Porto and later Fundação Porto Social and expanded its target area to include the whole city of Porto.

Disclosure statement

No potential conflict of interest was reported by the author(s).

References

Allegra, M., S. Tulumello, A. Colombo, and J. Ferrão. 2020. "The (Hidden) Role of the EU in Housing Policy: The Portuguese Case in Multi-scalar Perspective." *European Planning Studies* 28 (12): 2307–2329. doi:10.1080/09654313.2020.1719474.

Alves, S. 2008. "A diferença que a participação faz em iniciativas de regeneração urbana." *Sociedade e Território*, no. 41: 8–18.

Alves, S. 2013. "Evaluation and Evaluating the Community Initiative URBAN." In *2nd International Scientific Conference, Regional Development, Spatial Planning and Strategic Governance (RESPAG), 22–25 May*, 1–18. Belgrade: Institute of Architecture and Urban & Spatial Planning of Serbia.

Alves, S. 2017. "Assessing the Impact of Area-based Initiatives in Deprived Neighborhoods: The Example of S. João de Deus in Porto, Portugal." *Journal of Urban Affairs* 39 (3): 381–399. doi:10.1080/07352166.2016.1245081.

Alves, S., and R. Branco. 2018. "With or without You: Models of Urban Requalification under Neoliberalism in Portugal." In *Changing Societies: Legacies and Challenges. Vol. I. Ambiguous Inclusions: Inside Out, outside In*, edited by S. Aboim, P. Granjo, and A. Ramos, 457–479. Lisboa: Imprensa de Ciências Sociais.

Antalovsky, E., J. S. Dangschat, and M. Parkinson, eds. 2005. *European Metropolitan Governance Cities in Europe – Europe in the Cities. Final Report*. Vienna and Liverpool: Europaforum Wien, EFW, EIUA and ISRA.

Armstrong, H. 1995. "The Role and Evolution of European Community Regional Policy." In Jones, Barry and Keating, Michael(Eds.,)*The European Union and the Regions*, 23–64. Oxford: Oxford University Press.

Athanassiou, E. 2020. "Transferring Sustainability: Imaginaries and Processes in EU Funded Projects in Thessaloniki." *Urban Research & Practice* 1–22. doi:10.1080/17535069.2020.1783351.

Atkinson, R. 2001. "The Emerging 'Urban Agenda' and the European Spatial Development Perspective: Towards an EU Urban Policy?" *European Planning Studies* 9 (3): 385–406. doi:10.1080/09654310120037630.

Atkinson, R., and C. Rossignolo. 2010. "Cities and the 'Soft Side' of Europeanization: The Role of Urban Networks." In *The Europeanization of Cities. Policies, Urban Change & Urban Networks*, edited by A. Hamedinger and A. Wolffhardt, 193–206. Amsterdam: Techne Press.

Atkinson, R. 2015. "The Urban Dimension in Cohesion Policy: Past Developments and Future Prospects." *European Structural and Investment Funds Journal* 3 (1): 21–31.

Atkinson, R., and K. Zimmermann. 2016. "Cohesion Policy and Cities: An Ambivalent Relationship." In *Handbook on Cohesion Policy in the EU*, edited by S. Piattoni and L. Polverari, 413–426. Cheltenham: Edward Elgar.

Bachtler, J., and C. Mendez. 2007. "Who Governs EU Cohesion Policy? Deconstructing the Reforms of the Structural Funds." *JCMS: Journal of Common Market Studies* 45 (3): 535–564.

Bachtler, J., C. Mendez, and F. Wishlade. 2013. *EU Cohesion Policy and European Integration. The Dynamics of EU Budget and Regional Policy Reform*. London: Routledge.

Bachtler, J., M. Ferry, C. Méndez, and I. McMaster. 2006. "The 2007-13 Operational Programmes: A Preliminary Assessment." In *IQ-Net, Improving the Quality of Structural Funds Programming through Exchange of Experience, 15–17 January*. Antwerp: European Policies Research Centre, University of Strathclyde.

Balsas, C. J. L. 2004. "City Centre Regeneration in the Context of the 2001 European Capital of Culture in Porto, Portugal." *Local Economy: The Journal of the Local Economy Policy Unit* 19 (4): 396–410. doi:10.1080/0269094042000286873.

Balsas, C. J. L. 2007. "City Centre Revitalization in Portugal: A Study of Lisbon and Porto." *Journal of Urban Design* 12 (2): 231–259. doi:10.1080/13574800701306328.

Bandeirinha, J. A. 2007. *O Processo SAAL E a Arquitectura No 25 De Abril De 1974*. Coimbra: Imprensa da Universidade de Coimbra.

Börzel, T. A., and T. Risse. 2000. "When Europe Hits Home: Europeanization and Domestic Change." *European Integration Online Papers* 4 (15): 1–20.

Branco, R., and S. Alves. 2018. "Urban Rehabilitation, Governance, and Housing Affordability: Lessons from Portugal." *Urban Research & Practice* 13 (2): 157–179. doi:10.1080/17535069.2018.1510540.

Branco, R., and S. Alves. 2020. "Outcomes of Urban Requalification under Neoliberalism: A Critical Appraisal of the SRU Model." In Smagacz-Poziemska, MartaGómez, M. VictoriaPereira, PatríciaGuarino, LauraKurtenbach, SebastianVillalón, Juan JoséNot Started (Eds.,) *Inequality and Uncertainty*, 139–158. Singapore: Springer.

Breda-Vázquez, I., P. Conceição, and R. Fernandes. 2009. "Partnership Diversity and Governance Culture: Evidence from Urban Regeneration Policies in Portugal." *Urban Studies* 46 (10): 2213–2238. doi:10.1177/0042098009339433.

Breda-Vázquez, I., and S. Alves. 2004. "The Critical Role of Governance Structures in Oporto City-centre Renewal Projects." In *City Futures - International Conference in Globalization and Urban Change, EURA-UAA, 8-10 July*. Chicago: University of Illinois.

Câmara Municipal do Porto. 1998. *Relatório Final Projecto Piloto Urbano da Sé, Porto*. Porto: Câmara Municipal do Porto.

Câmara Municipal do Porto. 2015. *Plano Estrategico de Desenvolvimento Urbano do Porto. Versão da Candidatura Submetida ao Programa Operacional Regional Norte 2020. Setembro*. Porto: Câmara Municipal do Porto.

Câmara Municipal do Porto and PortoVivo. 2010. *Management Plan. Historic Centre of Porto World Heritage*. Porto: Câmara Municipal do Porto e Porto Vivo, SRU.

Campos, V., and J. Ferrão. 2015. "Ordenamento do Território em Portugal: Uma Perspectiva Genealógica." *ICS Working Papers*, no. 1.

Carpenter, J. 2006. "Addressing Europe's URBAN Challenges: Lessons from the EU URBAN Community Initiative." *Urban Studies* 43 (12): 2145–2162. doi:10.1080/00420980600990456.

Carpenter, J. 2010. "Integrated Urban Regeneration and Sustainability: Approaches from the European Union." In *Urban Regeneration and Social Sustainability: Best Practice from European Cities*, edited by A. Colantonio and T. Dixon, 83–101. Oxford: Wiley-Blackwell.

Carpenter, J. 2013. "Sustainable Urban Regeneration within the European Union: A Case of 'Europeanization'?" *The Routledge Companion to Urban Regeneration* 138–147.

Carpenter, J., M. G. Medina, M. Á. Huete García, and S. De Gregorio Hurtado. 2020. "Variegated Europeanization and Urban Policy: Dynamics of Policy Transfer in France, Italy, Spain and the UK." *European Urban and Regional Studies* 27 (3): 227–245. doi:10.1177/0969776419898508.

Carvalho, L., P. Chamusca, J. Rio Fernandes, and J. Pinto. 2019. "Gentrification in Porto: Floating City Users and Internationally-driven Urban Change." *Urban Geography* 40 (4): 565–572. doi:10.1080/02723638.2019.1585139.

Cavaco, C., R. Florentino, and A. Pagliuso. 2020. "Urban Policies in Portugal." In *Foregrounding Urban Agendas. The New Urban Issue in European Experiences of Policy-Making*, edited by S. Armondi and S. De Gregorio Hurtado, 49–72. Cham: Springer.

Chamusca, P. 2011. "Polis XXI, governância e planemanento urbano no norte de Portugal: Impactos do programa de Regeneração Urbana." In *Trunfos de uma Geografia Activa: Desenvolvimento Local, Ambiente, Ordenamento e Tecnologia*, edited by N. Santos and L. Cunha, 453–460. Coimbra: Imprensa da Universidade de Coimbra.

Costa, C., 2015. Quando nos (des) Envolvemos em Projetos de Desenvolvimento Local… Análise Crítica da Prática Profissional. Instituto Superior de Serviço Social do Porto

Costa, J. P. 2011. "Urban Rehabilitation Societies: The Oporto Case as a Reference in the Portuguese Practice." In *Bauhaus and the City: A Contested Heritage for A Challenging Future*, edited by L. Colini and F. Eckardt, 88–112. Wurzburg: Verlag Königshausen & Neumann.

Cotella, G. 2019. "The Urban Dimension of EU Cohesion Policy." In *Territorial Cohesion. The Urban Dimension*, edited by E. Medeiros, 133–151. Cham: Springer.

De Gregorio Hurtado, S. 2018. "The EU Urban Policy in the Period 2007–13: Lessons from the Spanish Experience." *Regional Studies, Regional Science* 5 (1): 212–230. doi:10.1080/21681376.2018.1480903.

De Gregorio Hurtado, S. 2019. "Understanding the Influence of EU Urban Policy in Spanish Cities: The Case of Málaga." *Urban Research & Practice* 1–26. doi:10.1080/17535069.2019.1690672.

Domingues, Á., N. Portas, and T. Sá Marques. 2007. "Portugal: Urban Policies or Policies with an Urban Incidence?" In *National Policy Responses to Urban Challenges in Europe*, edited by L. van den Berg, E. Braun, and J. van der Meer, 311–332. Aldershot: Ashgate.

Dossi, S. 2017. *Cities and the European Union: Mechanisms and Modes of Europeanisation*. Colchester: ECPR Press.

Dukes, T. 2008. "The URBAN Programme and the European URBAN Policy Discourse: Successful Instruments to Europeanize the URBAN Level?" *GeoJournal* 72 (1–2): 105–119. doi:10.1007/s10708-008-9168-2.

ECOTEC. 2010. *URBAN II Evaluation. Case Study: Porto–Gondomar. An Isolated Success Story?* Birmingham.

European Commission. 2003. *Ex-post Evaluation. Urban Community Initiative (1994–1999). Final Report*. Brussels. GHK on behalf of European Commission.

European Commission. 2008. *Fostering the Urban Dimension: Analysis of the Operational Programmes Co-financed by the European Regional Development Fund (2007-2013). Working Document of the DG for Regional Policy*. Brussels.

European Commission. 2010. *Ex Post Evaluation of URBAN II. Case Study: Porto – Gondomar. An Isolated Success Story? Ex-Post Evaluation of Cohesion Policy Programmes 2000–2006: The URBAN Community Initiative*. Brussels: Evaluation report.

European Commission. 2011. *Desenvolvimento Urbano Sustentável em Portugal: Uma Abordagem Integrada*. Brussels: DG Regio.

European Parliament. 2014. *The Role of Cities in Cohesion Policy 2014-2020*. Brussels: Publications Office of the European Union.

Faludi, A. 2014. "EUropeanisation or Europeanisation of Spatial Planning?" *Planning Theory and Practice* 15 (2): 155–169. doi:10.1080/14649357.2014.902095.

FDVC. 2001. *Urban do Vale de Campanhã. Relatório Final*. Porto: Fundação para o Desenvolvimento do Vale de Campanhã.

Featherstone, K., and C. M. Radaelli, eds. 2003. *The Politics of Europeanization*. Oxford: Oxford University Press.

Ferreira, V. M., and F. Indovina, eds. 1999. *A cidade da EXPO'98: uma reconversão na frente ribeirinha de lisboa?* Lisboa: Bizâncio.

Green Cowles, M., J. A. Caporaso, and T. Risse, eds. 2001. *Transforming Europe: Europeanization and Domestic Change*. Ithaca and London: Cornell University Press.

Gros, M. 1993. "Luta Contra a Exclusao Social: Assistencialismo Ou Desenvolvimento Local?" In *Estruturas Sociais e Desenvolvimento – Actas do II Congresso de Socologia*. Lisboa: Fragmentos.

Guerra, P. 2004. "O Bairro do Cerco do Porto: Cenários de Pertenças, de Afectividades e de Simbologias." In *V Congresso Português de Sociologia. Sociedades Contemporâneas: Reflexividade e Acção, 12-15 Maio*. Braga: Universidade do Minho, 51–56.

Hamedinger, A., and A. Wolffhardt, eds. 2010. *The Europeanization of Cities. Policies, Urban Change & Urban Networks*. Amsterdam: Techne Press.

Hooghe, L., ed. 1996. *Cohesion Policy and European Integration: Building Multi-Level Governance*. Oxford: Oxford University Press.

John, P. 2001. *Local Governance in Western Europe*. London: SAGE.

Le Galès, P. 2002. *European Cities. Social Conflicts and Governance*. New York: Oxford University Press.

Leonardi, R. 2005. "Cohesion Policy in the European Union: The Building of Europe." In *Cohesion Policy in the European Union*. Basingstoke and New York: Palgrave Macmillan.

Leonardi, R. 2006. "Cohesion in the European Union." *Regional Studies* 40 (2): 155–166. doi:10.1080/00343400600600462.

Liesbet, H., and G. Marks. 2001. *Multi-Level Governance and European Integration*. Oxford: Rowman & Littlefield.

Lobato, I. R., and S. Alves. 2012. "Urban Decay in Porto – Strengths and Weaknesses of Portuguese Regeneration Programmes." In *ENHR 2012 Conference: Housing: Local Welfare and Local Markets in a Globalised World. 24 to 27 June*. Lillehammer: European Network on Housing Research.

Magone, J. 2006. "The Europeanization of Portugal (1986–2006). A Critical View." *Nação E Defesa* 115 (3a Série): 9–28.

Mamede, L., and A. F. Tavares. 2010. "O Programa POLIS no processo de Governação Urbana." In *4° Congresso Luso-Brasileiro Para o Planejamento Urbano, Regional, Integrado, Sustentável (PLURIS): The Challenges of Planning in a Web Wide World, 6–8 Outubro*. Faro: Universidade do Algarve.

Marques, T. S., M. Saraiva, G. Santinha, and P. Guerra. 2018. "Re-Thinking Territorial Cohesion in the European Planning Context." *International Journal of Urban and Regional Research* 42 (4): 547–572. doi:10.1111/1468-2427.12608.

Marshall, A. 2005. "Europeanization at the Urban Level: Local Actors, Institutions and the Dynamics of Multi-level Interaction." *Journal of European Public Policy* 12 (4): 668–686. doi:10.1080/13501760500160292.

Medeiros, E. 2014. "The 'Europeanization of Spatial Planning Processes in Portugal within the EU Cohesion Policy Strategies (1989-2013)." *Geography and Spatial Planning Journal*, no. 6: 201–222. doi:10.17127/got/2014.6.012.

Medeiros, E., and A. van der Zwet. 2019. "Evaluating Integrated Sustainable Urban Development Strategies: A Methodological Framework Applied in Portugal." *European Planning Studies* 4313: 1–20.

Medina, M. G., and V. Fedeli. 2015. "Exploring European Urban Policy: Towards an EU-national Urban Agenda?" *Gestión Y Análisis De Políticas Públicas*, no. 14: 8–22.

Molle, W. 2007. *European Cohesion Policy*. London: Routledge.

Mourão, J. 2019. "Regeneração urbana integrada, proteção do património cultural e eficiência ambiental como objetivos divergentes nas políticas urbanas em Portugal (2000–2020)." *Cidades, Comunidades e Territórios*, no. 38: 79–95.

Neto, L., N. Pinto, and M. Burns. 2014. "Evaluating the Impacts of Urban Regeneration Companies in Portugal: The Case of Porto." *Planning Practice and Research* 29 (5): 525–542. doi:10.1080/02697459.2014.973685.

Oliveira, A., F. Ferreira, and R. Dias. 2019. "A Cidade (Euro)governável: Políticas e Instrumentos de Governação Urbana no Portugal 2020." In *Ativar Cidades. Modelos de Políticas de Cidades*, edited by P. C. Seixas, 39–53. Lisboa: Caleidoscópio.

Oliveira, C., and I. Breda-Vázquez. 2011. "Territorial Governance in Portugal: Institutional Change or Institutional Resilience?" *disP - the Planning Review* 47 (186): 64–76. doi:10.1080/02513625.2011.10557145.

Oliveira, C., and I. Breda-Vázquez. 2012. "Europeanisation of Territorial Policies in Portugal and Italy: A Cross-national Comparison." *Policy & Politics* 40 (1): 87–103. doi:10.1332/030557310X520261.

Oliveira, V., A. Martins, and S. S. Cruz. 2013. "Evaluating Urban Policies from a Resilience Perspective: The Case of Oporto." In *Resilience Thinking in Urban Planning*, edited by A. Eraydin and T. Taşan-kok, 161–178. Dordrecht: Springer.

Olsen, J. 2002. "The Many Faces of Europeanization." *Journal of Common Market Studies* 40 (5): 921–952. doi:10.1111/1468-5965.00403.

Parkinson, M., F. Bianchini, J. Dawson, R. Evans, and A. Harding, eds. 1992. *Regional Development. Studies. Urbanization and the Functions of Cities in the European Community*. Luxembourg: Office for Official Publications of the European Communities.

Piattoni, S., and L. Polverari, eds. 2016. *Handbook on Cohesion Policy in the EU*. Cheltenham: Edward Elgar.

Pinho, A. 2009. *Conceitos e Políticas Europeias de Reabilitação Urbana. Análise da experiência portuguesa dos Gabinetes Técnicos Locais*. Lisboa: Universidade Técnica de Lisboa.

Queirós, J. 2007. "Estratégias e discursos políticos em torno da reabilitação de centros urbanos: Considerações exploratórias a partir do caso do Porto." *Sociologia, Problemas e Praticas* 55 (1966): 91–116.

Queirós, J. 2013. "Precariedade habitacional, vida quotidiana e relação com o Estado no centro histórico do Porto na transição da ditadura para a democracia." *Análise Social* XLVIII (206): 102–133.

Queirós, M. 2014. "Desarrollo urbano sostenible en la agenda de cohesión territorial europea: Política de Ciudades Polis XXI, Portugal." *Perspectiva Geográfica* 18 (2): 303. doi:10.19053/01233769.2680.

Queirós, M., and M. Vale. 2005. "Ambiente Urbano e Intervenção Pública: O Programa POLIS." In *Comunicações do X Colóquio Ibérico de Geografia: A Geografia Ibérica no Contexto Europeu, 22 a 24 de Setembro*, 1–16. Évora: Universidade de Évora.

Radaelli, C. 2003. "The Europeanization of Public Policy." In *The Politics of Europeanization*, edited by K. Featherstone and C. M. Radaelli, 27–56. Oxford: Oxford University Press.

Ramsden, P., and L. Colini, eds. 2013. *Urban Development in the EU: 50 Projects Supported by the European Regional Development Fund during the 2007-13 Period*. Brussels: European Commission, Directorate General for Regional and Urban Policy.

Rio Fernandes, J. 2011. "Area-based Initiatives and Urban Dynamics. The Case of the Porto City Centre." *Urban Research & Practice* 4 (3): 285–307. doi:10.1080/17535069.2011.616747.

Rio Fernandes, J., F. Teles, P. Chamusca, and J. Seixas. 2020. "The Power of the Cities and the Power in the Cities: A Multiscale Perspective from Portugal." *Boletín de la Asociación de Geógrafos Españole*, no. 87. doi:10.21138/bage.2978.

Rosa, F., 2018. *O Desenvolvimento Urbano Sustentável na Política de Coesão. Working Paper No. 2*. Coleção Política e Territórios. Lisboa: Agência para o Desenvolvimento e Coesão, No. WP02.

Santos, Á., and M. Branco-Teixeira. 2020. "The Contribution of Tourism to the Renegeration of Cities: A Route for Change." *Worldwide Hospitality and Tourism Themes* 12 (6): 753–760. doi:10.1108/WHATT-07-2020-0074.

Seixas, P. C. 2008. *Entre Manchester e Los Angeles. Ilhas e novos condomínios no Porto: paradigmas sócio-espaciais, políticas da diferença e estruturas antropológicas urbanas*. Porto: Edições Universidade Fernando Pessoa.

Sequeira, J. P. 2011. "Ruptura(s) e Continuidade(s): A Reabilitação da Baixa e Centro Histórico do Porto." In *Diálogo Cultural entre Iberoamérica y Europa – Patrimonio Urbanístico Ilustrado: Experiencias y Proyectos en Brasil, Cuba, Guatemala, Portugal y España*, 63–73. Valencia: Associação Internacional de Cidades e Entidades do Iluminismo.

Sousa, S., and P. Pinho. 2016. "O planeamento de cidades em contração: o caso do Porto." *Boletim Regional, Urbano e Ambiental*, no. 14: 93–106.

Stewart, M. 1994. "Towards a European Urban Policy." *Local Economy* 9 (3): 266–277. doi:10.1080/02690949408726240.

Tofarides, M. 2003. *Urban Policy in the European Union: A Multi-Level Gatekeeper System*. Aldershot: Ashgate.

Tosics, I. 2016. "Integrated Territorial Investment. A Missed Opportunity?" In *EU Cohesion Policy: Reassessing Performance and Direction*, edited by J. Bachtler, P. Berkowitz, S. Hardy, and T. Muravska, 284–296. London: Routledge.

van den Berg, L., E. Braun, and J. van der Meer, eds. 2007. *National Policy Responses to Urban Challenges in Europe*. Aldershot: Ashgate.

Vinci, I. 2019. "How the EU Regional Policy Can Shape Urban Change in Southern Europe: Learning from Different Planning Processes in Palermo." *Urban Research & Practice* 1–26. doi:10.1080/17535069.2019.1672083.

Zerbinati, S. 2004. "Europeanization and EU Funding in Italy and England. A Comparative Local Perspective." *Journal of European Public Policy* 11 (6): 1000–1019. doi:10.1080/1350176042000298075.

Transferring sustainability: imaginaries and processes in EU funded projects in Thessaloniki

Evangelia Athanassiou

ABSTRACT
Since the 1990s, sustainability agenda has dominated cities' efforts to improve their environment; has been elaborated in European Commission documents, has been disseminated and funded through different mechanisms. The paper examines the way urban sustainability has been framed in Thessaloniki's EU funded urban regeneration projects, focusing on projects that have been materialized or planned, since the outbreak of the financial crisis in Greece in 2010. It places emphasis on conceptual shifts in EU policies regarding sustainability and their reflection on specific urban projects. A critical light is shed on imaginaries pursued, and processes employed in these projects.

Introduction

Cities, as both places of environmental degradation and appropriate terrains for environmental policies, have been at the core of European initiatives since the *Green paper on the Urban Environment* (CEC 1990). Since the 1990s, the urban sustainability agenda has dominated cities' efforts to improve their environment; it has been elaborated in successive European commission documents, has been disseminated through networks and has been funded through different EU mechanisms. A 'green' agenda for urban regeneration projects has also been promoted and has been infused into interventions in different scales ranging from zero-emission brownfield developments to climate adaptation through the redesign of squares and streets.

Thessaloniki, a city of the European South, representing the rigid, state controlled South European 'urbanism' tradition and located in one of EU's 'less developed regions' (ERDF 2014–2020), after successive programming periods of regional funding (ec. europa.eu) offers a good case study to investigate the ways through which dominant concepts of EU spatial policies are transferred to different urban contexts. Studying Thessaloniki, this paper seeks to address the following research questions: How are dominant paradigms of EU spatial policies transferred across different regions? More specifically, through what processes do mainstream imaginaries about the relationship between cities and nature become embedded in specific projects, in variegated urban environments?

To address the above research questions the paper embarks on an analysis of EU funded urban regeneration projects in Thessaloniki along two axes. The first axis of analysis identifies dominant conceptualizations of urban sustainability that are endorsed and promoted in the projects. The second axis studies the processes, through which these imaginaries infiltrate into local urban policies and become embedded into different urban environments.

The paper adopts a critical stance towards the way the relationship between cities and 'nature' has been formulated in mainstream environmentalism and has subsequently imbued policies at multiple scales, from the supra-national to the local. In doing so, the paper is inspired by the urban political ecology literature and the conceptualization of cities as socio-natural entities in constant flux and not as technical entities degrading pristine 'nature' (Smith 2006). Urban sustainability is understood as a multi-level governance pursuit (Bulkeley and Betsill 2005), constantly formulated in a local, national, European and global context and not as isolated local adaptations of the naturalised 'urban ecosystem' to planetary emergencies.

In a similar vein, urban regeneration policies are not perceived, in this paper, as static and fixed processes determined by national frameworks, but as constantly constituted in a path dependent and multi-level manner involving many actors in non-hierarchical networks (Reimer, Getimis, and Blotevogel 2014). Having this in mind, the paper sets out to discuss the way urban sustainability has been framed in Thessaloniki'sEU funded urban regeneration projects, focusing on projects that have been materialized or planned in the city since the outbreak of the latest financial crisis in Greece in 2010. It analyses EU urban policies and their transfer to a South European context, shedding a critical light on imaginaries endorsed, goals pursued and processes employed. First, the paper traces discursive shifts in the way urban sustainability is conceptualized in EU policy documents. Subsequently, it identifies the influence of these hegemonic conceptualizations on the formal structure of spatial planning in Greece, at a national level. The paper then focuses on lower levels of governance – most notably the municipal – and the ways EU conceptualisations of sustainability have been embedded on urban regeneration projects.

Europeanisation of urban policies and governance, of a country of the European South, is inevitably a parallel theme in this analysis. As Andreou (2006) points out 'the implementation of cohesion policy has not been simply a response to 'European' prescriptions, but the outcome of a continuous interaction between a great numbers of actors, be they supranational, national and subnational institutions or domestic interest groups' (ibid.). He goes on to examine 'Europeanization' as 'a bottom-up' process. In other words, notwithstanding its transformative effect on national institutional structures and policy priorities, Europeanisation, just like neoliberalisation, is not a fixed regime that is transposed unaltered to different member states. There is no 'textbook' Europeanisation. Rather it is a continuous dialectic encounter between hegemonic EU agendas and diversified local contexts. It is argued that austerity politics imposed by the 'troika' since 2010 have played a catalyzing role, in accelerating Europeanisation of spatial policies at a national level in Greece, and, in transforming imaginaries of urban sustainability and models of urban governance, at city level.

Research is based on EU policy documents and official sites, Greek planning legislation, and the Greek ESDP official site, as well as actual projects' rationale and stated objectives.

Changing imaginaries and predominant themes of sustainability in EU policy documents

In order to identify how sustainability has been transferred to urban projects in Thessaloniki, it is necessary to trace its trajectory in EU urban policy. Key policy documents are analysed with regard to their conceptualization of sustainability. This section seeks to highlight predominant themesandunveil conceptual shifts in this trajectory.

The *Green paper for the Urban environment* (CEC 1990) was the first European Commission document that placed cities at the core of environmental problems and introduced a clear urban dimension to environmental policies. It was issued three years only after the Brundtland report (WCED 1987) and greatly enhanced European Commission's environmental policies, which were, until then, strictly sectoral. The *Green Paper* stressed cities' impact on their immediate environment as well as their contribution to planetary problems, mainly to the 'greenhouse effect'. The city was thus conceptualized as a manmade entity degrading the natural environment, which was understood in the document as a separate entity with its own value and eternal processes. The age-old separation between nature and society was thus fully endorsed and reproduced (Smith 1984). Nature within cities was identified with parks, gardens and urban wildlife.

The *Green paper* suggested that '[h]owever diverse in detail, Europe's major cities face common problems' (CEC 1990). Examining the 'root causes' of urban problems of the 'European city', it recognized functionalism and strict zoning of land uses as inspired by the *Athens Charter* of 1933, among them. It also recognized common areas of action that had to do both with the physical structure of the city and the impact of urban activities on the environment. In terms of urban form, the *Green Paper* promoted the compact city model, sidelining the fact that European cities differ greatly in terms of urbanization processes, planning systems and urban forms. Strict land use zoning, low-density suburbanization, and degraded social housing complexes, portrayed as features of the 'european city' were not major problems of cities of the European South (Hastaoglou-Martinidis, Kalogirou, and Papamichos 1993). Moreover, spatial features like high density and mixture of uses, promoted in the *Paper* as solutions, constituted problematic features of Greek urban fabrics. Considering both the projected problems and their 'root causes', it appears that the 'european city' was discursively constructed to correspond to the Western and central European city, which had been strongly impacted by industrialization and deindustrialization and their planning systems hadlargelytakenon board the tenets of modern urban planning (Athanassiou 2000).

As regards to the relationship between environmental protection and market economy, the *Green paper* states: «[The] conflict between environment and economy is … a false one, since in the long term the protection of the environmental resources is a basic condition for sustained economic growth, which can itself contribute to environmental improvement». The document echoes the neomalthusian idea of 'limits to growth' (Meadows et al. 1972) and suggests that environmental protection is necessary, not for nature's sake, or for ethical reasons, but because nature constitutes the finite material framework of human development.

Among the instruments suggested towards addressing the problems of the 'european city' are information initiatives, which are specified in 'the creation of a network of urban local inititiatives'. The EC, the *Paper* suggested, should support cities in their effort to become sustainable. Funds would be channeled through European Regional Policy in particular action areas within Objectives 1&2. Forty percent of European cities were within the scope of these Objectives (CEC, 37). Although a policy addressed to regions, the *Green paper* suggested it could be utilized for urban environments.

Since 1990, there has been a lot of activity in promoting urban sustainability through funding, network building and research. This corresponded to an era of sustained economic growth and increased interest in the spatial dimensions of common European policy. Sixteen years after the Green Paper, the Thematic strategy on the urban environment (Official Journal of the EU, 2006) did not endorse a specific spatial form, but urged cities to prioritize 'projects limiting greenfield and promoting brown-field developments, and to promote the planting of street trees and designation of more green space' (EC 2006a, 184). It also stressed the significance of monitoring, networking and exchange of 'best practice'. Sustainability, in management, transport and planning, was the dominant concept and resilience was not yet among the goals for European cities. However, the need to manage environmental risks triggered by climate change was mentioned in this strategy. The same document recognized the role of a high-quality urban environment to promote 'the priority of the Lisbon strategy to "make Europe attractive to work and investment"'. Attractiveness of cities 'will enhance their potential for growth and job creation'. Hence, the neomalthusian strand of environmentalism, endorsed in the Green Paper, has been replaced in the Thematic Strategy by the 'ecological modernization' approach, which acquired prominence in the environmental politics discourse during the 1990s (seeMol, Sonnerfeld, and Spaargaren 2009). Ecological modernization, as it consolidated in 'sustainable development' and 'green economy', sustains that there is no conflict between environmental protection and growth. Quite the contrary, the two can be mutually supportive. This approach opened up the environment as a fertile ground for capital accumulation, supported by scientific discourse.

The outbreak of the latest capitalist crisis of 2008 corresponds to the dominance of a new integrating concept for cities, namely urban resilience. Resilience has complemented sustainability in EU and other international organizations' policy documents. In 2013, the *7th Action plan for the environment* was entitled 'Living well, within the limits of our planet' (EC 2013) recalling again the Neomalthusian*Limits to Growth* of the Club of Rome (Meadows et al 1972) and other publications of the early 1970s which stressed the idea of natural limits to human development. All stated 'priorities' of the *Action Plan* are strictly environmental, namely 'to protect nature and strengthen ecological resilience, boost resource-efficient, low-carbon growth, and reduce threats to human health and wellbeing linked to pollution, chemical substances, and the impacts of climate change' (ibid, 2). In this document, resilience was endorsed as a feature of economy, society and nature. Within the *7th*

Action plan, action was presented as urgent and did not aim only at mitigation of cities' impact on planetary environmental problems, but also at adaptation to 'emerging environmental and climate risks' (EC 2013). Nature, thus, was still presented as a separate entity to society, but lost its eternal and harmonious function and was construed as already destabilized by human development, fraught with unpredictable 'risks', 'threats' and 'pressures'. Nations and cities were urged to adapt to these risks.

The new resilience discourse sustained and enhanced the 'ecological modernization' rhetoric, complementing it with a sense of urgency, supported by scientific data. Environmental risks, economic instability and social unrest construed a 'state of emergency' for cities worldwide and compelled them to forge mitigation and adaptation strategies. These strategies were also expected to boost cities' economies. Predominant themes among suggested actions were monitoring, to 'increase knowledge base' as well as 'adequate investments and innovation in products, services and public policies [...] from public and private sources' (ibid 3).

A clear shift can be recorded. While in the *Green paper*, protection of environmental resources was identified as 'a basic condition for sustained economic growth', in the *7th Action plan*, 'concerted action should be taken now to improve ecological resilience and maximize the benefits environment policy can deliver for the economy and society ... '. Also, 'action to mitigate and adapt to climate change will increase the resilience of the Union's economy and society, while stimulating innovation and protecting the Union's natural resources' (EC 2013).

EU ways to make 'our cities attractive and sustainable' (EC 2010) have become much more varied than in the 1990s. Networking to exchange 'best practices' has gradually acquired a pivotal role. Already in 2002, the URBACT programme strengthened the urban dimension of regional funds and could be utilized by all cities of the EU to connect to each other and exchange experience. Acknowledging the diversity of urban environments within the EU and marking a clear break with earlier imaginaries of common problems and solutions for the 'european city', URBACT III states that it 'will respect the diversity of European settlement system and will target all kinds of European cities and towns including smaller and medium sized cities' (EU 2014, 11). The Covenant of Mayors was launched in 2008, to promote exchange of experience between local authorities with regard to climate and energy. As the initiative's site boasts: the key success factors of the initiative [are] its bottom-up governance, its multi-level cooperation model and its context-driven framework for action (www.covenantofmayors.eu).

Overall, in the course of time since the *Green paper*, there has been a notable strengthening of the urban dimension of EU policies and funding. Reaching the current 2014–2020 period, member states are obliged to earmark at least 5% of their national Strategic Reference Framework (NSRF) to support integrated sustainable urban development strategies, addressing economic, environmental, climate, demographic and social challenges (EC 2016). However, estimates suggest a much higher percentage will be addressed to urban development projects (Medeiros and Van der Zwet 2019). Urban authorities are directly responsible for managing and implementing programmes of this period with a view to empowering municipalities and regional governments. Moreover, there has been a major shift on the very *rationale* of urban policies in the EU. As stated in the 'State of the European cities 2016':

> For long time cities were seen as a problem rather than a potential. Urban policies in Europe, for instance, were mostly focused on problems of poverty, crime and urban decay. [.]. Cities today, however, are increasingly recognized for their economic, social and environmental potential. As a result, urban policies are expanding their scope to ensure these benefits are fully expoited (EU& UN 2016, 11).

At the same time, the environmental dimension of EU funding mechanisms has been significantly strengthened, diversified and refashioned to promote 'adaptation to climate change'. For the current programming period (2014–2020) at least 20% of EU budget will be directed towards 'climate action' (EU 2016, 172).

Summing up, EU support for sustainable urban development has been gaining ground in policy documents and funding mechanisms. Urban nature, identified in the *Green Paper* with urban greenery, has been extended to include issues of urban metabolism, social equity and economic development. Urban sustainability in EU policy documents, however, has been conceptualized on the basis of a traditional divide between city and nature, foregrounding planetary problems and discourses of natural boundaries to human development as originally propagated in the 1970s. Resilience has complemented sustainability and has introduced an increasing sense of emergency and risk to urban development. Nature, in the resilience discourse, is not the benign and predictable entity that 'urban ecosystems' need to imitate, but rather the modified and unstable entity to which cities need to adapt. Within this framework, key themes related to sustainability in EU policy documents are the need for networking and exchange of 'best practices' between diverse urban environments, the requirement for innovative technical solutions and monitoring as responses to planetary problems and the inextricable, mutually supportive relationship between environmental protection and economic growth. Changing imaginaries about nature, emphasis on networking and technological innovation and on the growth potential of environmental protection have filtered through national planning and environmental frameworks, and local initiatives to different urban contexts across the EU. The following sections identify predominant imaginaries of sustainability in the Greek national planning framework and local urban regeneration projects in Thessaloniki.

Urban regeneration and the urban environment in the Greek planning system

Within the national planning systems of EU member-states, Greece, along with other Mediterranean countries is often classified to the 'urbanism tradition', because of its emphasis on issues of physical planning. It also has a strong regulatory character dominated by the central state, mostly regulating development rights of private land (EC 1997; Giannakourou 2005). This rigid formal tradition contrasts the strategic – 'non-binding procedural flexible'- character of EU spatial policy and leads to what Giannakourou (2005, 320) calls 'institutional misfit'. Nevertheless, as Getimis and Giannakourou point out, such classification mostly refers to Greek planning until the 1990s and does not take into account 'the dynamics and contradictions of ongoing planning agendas, the directions of change, the main driving forces and the new challenges in spatial planning discourses and practices' (2014, 151). The influence of EU policies since the 1990s and the financial crisis after 2010 have been two significant drives of change for the Greek planning system at the national level. This section follows changes at this level of planning with regard to the urban environment and urban regeneration.

The concept of sustainable development was first introduced in the Greek planning system by Law 2508/1997 'Sustainable development of cities and settlements'. Ten years after its most widely accepted definition in the Brundtland Report (WCED 1987), the law foregrounded the concept, as the central goal of urban development and suggested directions towards it. Reflecting a traditional understanding of planning, these directions included environmental and social goals, but made no reference to economic development. Regarding urban form, the law wholeheartedly adopted the 'compact city' model, as promoted by the EU since 1990. Henceforth, the model has been consistently incorporated in the rhetoric of local urban development plans, despite the fact that greek cities rank high among the most densely developed cities in Europe.

The same law introduced the concept of urban regeneration in the Greek planning system and the tools and mechanisms for urban interventions (Article 8). New tools aimed at 'the improvement of the urban environment, protection and promotion of cultural historic morphological and aesthetic features'. Urban areas eligible for intervention were to have one or more of the following characteristics: a) high densities and remarkable lack of public open spaces and social infrastructure b) incongruities between land uses c) lack of protection framework for their historic, archeological and cultural features and activities d) growing degradation of the aesthetics and quality of the built environment and natural elements. Reproducing the traditional divide between nature and the city, the law identifies nature with 'natural elements' which have been degraded by human activities such as unauthorized building or waste disposal. Development in terms of economic growth is not mentioned among the interventions' objectives (Government Newsletter 1997).

The law's focus on rather traditional objectives of urban interventions suggests a low level of Europeanisation at the time and a marked gap with EU's discursive priorities. This discursive gap however was soon to be overcome. Law 2742/1999 'Spatial planning and sustainable development' aimed at: 'the introduction of fundamental principles and the institutionalization of instruments, processes and means of implementation of spatial planning that promote sustainable and balanced development, establish productive and social cohesion, secure the protection of the environment [...] and strengthen the position of the country in the international and European context' (Government Newsletter 1999). Hence, the law introduced spatial planning as a means towards competitiveness in a European and global context.

Among the new means introduced by this law were the 'Projects of Integrated Urban Interventions' (PIUIs) (Article 10) which sought to promote 'integrated strategies of urban design in cities and urban areas that present composite problems of developmental delay, social and economic cohesion, environmental degradation and quality of life'. Transferring the multi-faceted spirit of sustainable development, PIUIs are seen as a significant terrain for 'the overall social, economic, environmental and cultural regeneration of cities'. The metaphor of the 'city as an ecosystem' is also transcribed from EU policy documents (EC 1996). PIUIs, however, were not to be activated until 2015 when the first such intervention was planned for the centre of Athens, which suffered major transformations during the crisis. Indeed, the Athens PIUIs included among its more traditional strategic directions – e.g. spatial and social cohesion and public space management – the strengthening of competitiveness and promotion of the city as a tourist destination. It also pledged to adopt 'innovative and contemporary forms of information management, smart city' and, to 'engage all actors, public and private, to the project's implementation' (Government Newsletter 2015).

During the 1990s, the Greek national planning legislation incorporated the concept of sustainability embracing gradually the different imaginaries that had been developed in relevant EU documents. Even the compact city model, as first suggested in the *Green Paper*, was endorsed, despite its limited relevance to the Greek urban context. In terms of governance, the regional tier was introduced in 1986 responding to the European mandate to manage funds regionally. Nevertheless, the planning system remained rigid, dominated by the central state and lacking strategic perspective.

Urban sustainability in the context of crisis

Since the outbreak of the financial crisis, in Greece the entire set of elsewhere-practiced neoliberal policies were tested on a new terrain and employed in a context-specific way (Brenner and Theodore 2002; Harvey 2006). Privatization of public land, natural resources and infrastructure, abolition of labour laws, and shrinkage of the public sector and public expenditure formed the core of successive 'memoranda' aimed at raising revenue for paying the national debt and creating a favourable 'business climate'.

Urban and non-urban land was not a mere field on which policies were implemented, but a key factor in this process. Key development policies introduced, since 2010, explicitly strove to make land more attractive to investment. Privatization and development of public land were among the stated axes of the national strategy towards recovery and were managed by the Hellenic Republic Asset Development Fund (HRADF), which had been specially created in July 2011 and re-instituted by the left SYRIZA government as the 'Hyper-fund' in 2015 (Vitopoulou and Yiannakou 2018).

Environmental protection was constituted in seemingly contradictory and diverting ways in the public realm: on the one hand, it was presented as an obstacle to economic growth and, on the other, it was promoted as the driving force of 'green development'. With regard to urban planning policy, the pursuit of urban sustainability, which filtered into national planning legislation through the above presented pieces of legislation in 1997 and 1999, was severely challenged, during the crisis. 'Planning reform' was among the country's obligations, clearly stated in the Second Economic Adjustment Programme for Greece (2012), imposed by the 'troika' of the International Monetary Fund, the European Commission and the European Central Bank. According to this *Second Memorandum of Understanding*, among other 'growth-enhancing reforms', the government should 'review and amend general planning and land-use legislation ensuring more flexibility in land development for private investment, and the simplification and acceleration of land-use plans'. To this direction, planning institutions, regulatory frameworks and urban development plans, as developed since the 1980s in the country, were presented in the public discourse as impediments to the development of private property, and hence, were to be by-passed, or altogether abolished. As part of the national strategy for recovery, since 2010, the pre-existing urban planning framework was first framed as a complicated backward mechanism causing unnecessary delays and hindering growth and, then, systematically relativized.

New planning laws, issued in 2014 and 2016, set the new framework of spatial planning, introducing what Pagonis and Karadimitriou (2019, 11–12) call 'exemptionary planning', i.e. a new 'pathway' of land development that circumvents existing local development plans and is directly controlled by the central government. This new 'pathway' is facilitated by new tools and processes that seek to render private and public land more attractive to private investment. They also introduce strategic planning, addressing the aforementioned 'institutional misfit' with EU spatial policies, and advancing Europeanization of the national planning system. Sustainability remained central in the new laws' objectives.

At the same time, since 2010, environmental protection and the concept of sustainable development were often activated in the official rhetoric to legitimize policies and projects, that adhere to 'ecological modernization', developing a rhetoric of 'green development'. The 'green dimension' of urban development became prevalent in recent local strategies and urban regeneration projects in Athens and Thessaloniki. Filtering EU guidelines into local governance, urban regeneration with an environmental agenda was seen as a means to improve the image of the city thus, making it more competitive in the world economy and more attractive to tourists and investors. Notwithstanding the integrative nature of sustainability and its prevalence in the official rhetoric, the concept was stripped from its original social dimension and became part of the pervasive urban competitiveness agenda. EU funding and networking mechanisms formed one level only in this multi-level constitution of strategies and specific projects towards urban sustainability. International and local charitable foundations, international actors, like the World Bank, interacted with local actors and institutions to reshape crisis-stricken cities towards green futures.

While new actors were introduced, a number of state organizations were abolished as part of the requirement for 'less state'. A crucial institution for the coordination of local authorities and projects at a metropolitan level, namely the *Organization of the Strategic Plan of Thessaloniki* was abolished in 2014. The *Organization* was founded in 1985, with a view to overlooking projects and policies towards the implementation of the city's *Strategic Urban Plan* (*RythmistikoThessalonikis*). The necessary update of this plan was commissioned in 2007, presented to public consultation in 2011, but was never ratified. A metropolitan area comprising 12 municipalities was left with no overarching strategy and no coordinating planning authority.

EU funded sustainable urban regeneration in Thessaloniki

Thessaloniki is the second biggest city in Greece, with a population of just over a million inhabitants (census 2011). The densely built urban conglomeration located along the coast of Thermaikos Bay, in the Northern part of the country, comprises 7 municipalities. The Municipality of Thessaloniki, which is the main focus of this paper, is the central and most populous of all. The Municipality boasts a vibrant historic centre and a long seafront that has been recently partly refashioned.

The first urban regeneration projects funded by the EU in Thessaloniki were planned and materialized in the beginning of the 1990s. Reflecting EU discursive transitions and funding priorities, those first EU funded interventions centered around promotion of the city's historic character, on the one hand, and social cohesion, on the other. They did not have a stated sustainability objective.

Municipality of Thessaloniki utilized the opportunity offered by the ERDF to fund 'studies or pilot projects to tackle urban problems'.The 'Urban Pilot Project for Renewal and Development of the Historic Commercial centre of Thessaloniki' funded by 75% by ERDF, was approved in 1991 and was implemented until 1996. It was a multifaceted project which targeted an area of approximately 17 Ha in the city's historic centre, which covers roughly 230 Ha, in total. The project aimed at restoring the historic fabric of the target area, for cultural and tourist uses, and at stimulating traditional and new economic activities. Towards these ends, it embarked on a series of interventions including restoration of historic buildings and monuments, pedestrianization and refashioning of public spaces, upgrading of infrastructure networks as well as institutional changes. 'The overall objective' as stated in the official ERDF site, was 'to improve the competitiveness of the city and to strengthen its position in the wider Balkan area, by encouraging further development, economic activity and international investment in the city' (https://ec.europa.eu/regional_policy). Planning and implementation of the Pilot project involved national, regional and local levels of governance and attracted private investment in the area. The project, although not fully implemented, had a strong and lasting impact in the city centre in physical terms. However, a large part of the target area, namely the historic wholesale area next to the city port, called Ladadika, was swiftly transformed into a tourist quartier exclusively occupied by restaurants and bars and no control over land uses was implemented (Image 1). Urban sustainability had only recently been introduced in the EU policy documents, and hence there was little, if any, stated environmental targeting in that project. With hindsight, of course, recycling of building stock and traffic arrangements restricting car traffic in the area can be seen as having a positive environmental impact.

Roughly the same period, the first URBAN project (1994–1999) was implemented in the Western districts of Thessaloniki. It included many small interventions in 4 Municipalities, namely Evosmou, Menemenis, Polichnis and Stavroupolis, covering an area of 1447 Ha. The project sought to address the lack of social infrastructure of a large urban area, characterized by high unemployment rates, phenomena of social exclusion and increased levels of pollution. However, it also undertook interventions on a degraded urban stream and an ex-military camp as well as on existing parks and squares. The project was managed by the *Organization of the Strategic Plan of Thessaloniki*and implemented by the Municipalities. The private sector also participated. Although urban sustainability had not yet filtered into national legislation, the URBAN initiative appears to have adopted an integrated approach, encompassing all three pillars of sustainable development and a novel model of urban governance, fostering coordination between local actors, be they public or private.

Finally, in 1997, Thessaloniki was awarded the title of European Capital of Culture and this cultural 'atypical mega event' (Deffner and Labrianidis 2005) was

Image 1. Pedestrianisations and reuse of historic buildings in ladadika district.

accompanied by a large Technical Programme. This, apart from projects upgrading the city's cultural infrastructure, comprised a number of urban regeneration projects, scattered in the city. Indeed, 43.1% of the budget of the Technical Programme went to urban regeneration aiming at the aesthetic upgrade of public spaces and the enhancement of the city's historic character (ibid.)With regards to urban interventions, the Municipality and other local and national actors involved did not adhere to the dominant paradigm of urban regeneration in Europe, namely the construction of iconic 'flagship projects', to create attractive urban images and often, specialized cultural services with an international appeal. On the contrary, there was a plethora of small scale unconnected urban regeneration projects. This constellation of projects did not form part of any stated urban strategy or coherent agenda aiming at sustainability. It was, however, supervised by the *Organization of the Strategic Plan of Thessaloniki* which looked into the projects' adherence to the 1985 *Strategic Plan's* objectives (Papadopoulos 2001).

All three projects, discussed above, involved a number of national, regional and local public authorities in their management and implementation.

Startingreluctantly, at the first decade of the 2000s, with the extensive refashioning of the New Waterfront, and, most notably after 2010, urban regeneration projects of various scales were planned and implemented, incorporating environmental dimensions either as technical requirements or, increasingly, as a central *rationale*. The following projects (Diagram 1) are the main EU projects undertaken since the 2000s and are indicative of the way sustainability has been framed in urban regeneration. They do not constitute an exhaustive record. Their analysis is based on the projects' rationale as developed in official local and European documents. Predominant themes of EU imaginaries of sustainability, as presented earlier in this paper, namely (1)

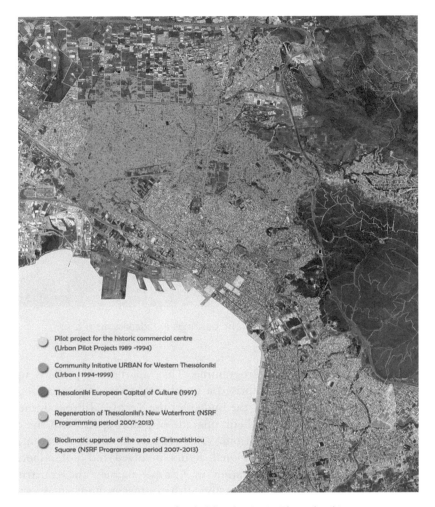

Diagram 1. Major regeneration projects funded by the EU in Thessaloniki.

urban greenery as 'nature in the city', (2) the importance of networking between diverse European urban contexts, (3) adaptiveness to planetary challenges and (4) financial sustainability are identified in the projects' rationale, separately or in combinations.

Refashioning the waterfront: sustainable as green

The newly refashioned New Waterfront of Thessaloniki is a wide urban promenade along the sea, featuring a bicycle lane and lined with a chain of eight thematic parks. It stretches on just over 3,2 km, along the part of the city that lies to the east of the city centre. The project was designed by a local architectural practice (Nikiforidis& Cuomo in collaboration with Atelier R. Castro – S. Denissof), who won a European architectural competition in 2001. The project was constructed in two phases between 2006 and 2014 and was managed by the Municipality of Thessaloniki, who had also launched the competition. It was co-funded by the NSRF in the programming period 2007–2013, as part of the Operational Programme 'Macedonia-Trace' – one of the 13 regional programmes of the NSF. The refashioning of the New Waterfront was the most expensive project in the region in the 'environment' axis for that programming period.

As stated at the NSRFofficial website (www.espa.gr) the benefits of this project are 'enhancement of the supralocal character of the area and its function as an attraction for citizens and visitors. Connection of the new waterfront to the urban fabric, that maintains and highlights the ecological character of the area, and enhancing its function as a green lung'.

The project's architectural quality has been widely acclaimed and has received a number of international awards (Image 2). Since its completion, the refashioned New Waterfront has been promoted as far more than a refurbished green public space. Rather, it is discursively constructed by the local press and EU official sites, as 'a jewel in the city's crown' (europa.eu), a new attractive image of the city to the world. The following quote is indicative:

> Thessaloniki, not only has a space that pushes it to escape from its Balkan misery, but at the same time it was bequeathed a project that teaches aesthetics to its citizens, everyday (https://www.protagon.gr/apopseis/blogs/efxaristoume-kyrie-nikiforidi-36659000000).

Notwithstanding its architectural quality and its success as a vivid public space, a number of questions can be raised regarding its overall impact on the city. First, the project was not, connected in any way to the bordering urban fabric which is separated from the waterfront by a six-lane arterial road, that connects the city centre to the suburban expanses to the east. The project did not include any traffic arrangements or traffic management, land use amendments or any other intervention to forge connections with the bordering residential area and allow for a better diffusion of its social and environmental benefits to the city's densely built fabric.

Moreover, the refurbished area is part of a much longer waterfront of around 54 km, that stretches along the metropolitan area, comprising natural beaches, areas of diffuse urbanization, areas of environmental degradation and touristic development, natural wetlands as well as transport infrastructure of regional importance, i.e. the city port and the airport. The refashioned part of the waterfront belongs to the central municipality of a metropolitan coastline that stretches along seven municipalities in total. There was no strategic goal to connect to the rest of the coastline.

Finally, there was no funding allocated to the maintenance of the renewed part, which already faces problems of degradation. Citizen initiatives have developed to address the lack of maintenance as well as enliven the place with cultural events.

'Greenness' in the case of the New Waterfront is identified with vegetation in the parks develop alongside the promenade. The idea of 'nature in the city', as first construed in the *Green paper*, is transferred in Thessaloniki as highly visible, attractive and quantifiable – number of trees, m^2 of parks – greenery. This restricted view of the environment excludes socio-natural processes and constructs nature as a quantifiable 'thing' with fixed boundaries and an attractive image that can be inserted to a man-made urban environment. It thus reproduces the age-old separation of society and nature that permeates mainstream expressions of environmentalism and EU's framing of the urban environment. The New Waterfront has been utilized as an 'uploadable' urban intervention, projecting its prestigious design and its role as a 'green lung'. It is published in the Covenant of Mayors' site, as a 'best practice' for European cities.[1]

Climatic upgrade of Chrimatistiriou Square: sustainable as adaptive to climate change

The «bioclimatic upgrade» of the area of Chrimatistiriou square was also funded by the NSRF in the same programming period (2007–2013). It was part of the axis 'Environment – Sustainable development' and was managed by the Municipality of Thessaloniki. The project aimed at addressing the Urban Heat Island and improving microclimatic conditions in part of the historic commercial centre. The project area is 12 Ha and comprises a formerly commercial area that has been degraded and recently gentrified. It represents the most popular nightlife quarter in the city with numerous bars and restaurants, while former retail and wholesale commercial uses and workshops are rapidly being eliminated.

The project involved the installation of fountains and water jets for cooling through evaporation, big outdoor fans to facilitate air movement, cool paving materials (Image 3). Pedestrianizations and traffic calming arrangements have been implemented and two new squares have been created on sites formerly used as car parks. Expected outcomes are the reduction of air temperature in summer days by 3°C, energy savings related to reduced cooling load for buildings and reduction of CO_2 emissions by 156 tonnes/year. The 'upgrade' of the area is also expected to 'boost commercial activities,

Image 2. The refashioning of the New Waterfront.

Image 3. Climatic upgrade of Chrimatistiriou Square.

increase the sense of safety and contribute to the promotion of history and cultural heritage'. Increased accessibility and the creation of a 'cultural route' are also mentioned (http://nws.eurocities.eu/MediaShell/media/CoM_Thessaloniki_EL.pdf).The rehabilitation of historic buildings is mentioned as an action that would be undertaken by the private sector. The project did not comprise any land use policy or other measures to safeguard existing renters or businesses.

Environmental upgrading with an emphasis on improving the microclimate during summer months becomes the definitive axis of this EU funded project and the ground on which its funding was vindicated. Issues like enhancing the area's historic character or reclaiming public space from car traffic are anchored to the central climate adaptation rationale, which is pursued through prominent technological devices. Reflecting shifts in EU imaginaries of nature, this project identifies nature as planetary and modified by human actions and sustainability as strictly environmental, technologically pursued and quantifiable.

The project was inaugurated in March 2016 and it is 'uploaded' as a 'good practice' at the Covenant of Mayors official site. Reduction of CO_2 emissions is the only outcome mentioned.

The shift to resilience: sustainable as networked

The concept of resilience first filtered into the vocabulary of the municipality through its participation to the '100 Resilient Cities' network of the Rockefeller Foundation (www.100resilientcities.org) and through its participation to the Resilient Europe network funded by URBACT III, since 2016.URBACT is a 'know-how programme' promoting capacity building, collaboration and exchange of experience between cities.

URBACT III (2014-2020) enhances the same objective, and aims 'promote sustainable integrated urban development' (URBACT 2017, 2). It is indicative of the programme's nature that 52% of its funding is for networking activities and does not support pilot projects. Funding is directly aimed at municipalities.

The Municipality of Thessaloniki collaborated with nine cities in the field of 'Urban environment and resilience' and the thematic axis of 'Promoting sustainable transport and removing bottlenecks in key network infrastructures'. The project for Thessaloniki aims at promoting cycling and developing a cycling culture in the city. An *Action Plan* was created towards this end in 2018 (Municipality of Thessaloniki, 2018). The *Plan* suggests extending the existing, limited and largely unused, network of cycle lanes in the whole Municipality and identifies connections with bordering municipalities with a view to constructing a metropolitan network. Following European guidelines, and aligned with predominant conceptualizations of resilience, the Municipality embraced citizen participation as part of this project. A process of citizen participation was organized in Toumba, a neighborhood to the east of the city centre. This was, however, an one-off experiment, with doubtful outcomes. In fact, participation has been sidelined or severely restricted in the national planning system, as part of the recent planning reform and the pledge to increase efficiency and remove impediments to development.

It should be noted that the *Action plan* vindicates itself on the basis a strategic goal stated at 'Resilient Thessaloniki: A Strategy for 2030' (City of Thessaloniki 2016) which is an outcome of the municipality's participation at the 100 Resilient Cities network. That strategy, however, does not have any institutional authorization within the domestic planning system and is not binding in any way. Overall, it can be observed that, while URBACT networks promote connections between diverse European urban contexts, Thessaloniki's project remains disconnected from its domestic planning system.

Towards energy efficiency: sustainable as revenue producing

The last case presented here is an 'urban development project' which aims to reduce energy consumption for street lighting. The Municipality activated a new EU mechanism for funding urban development projects, namely JESSICA (Joint European Support for Sustainable Investment in City Areas), to replace lighting in 43 streets with energy efficient led lamps. This 'urban development project' involved no other intervention.

JESSICA was introduced in the 2007–2013 programming period and, as the official website of the European Union suggests, its 'implementation entails a profound cultural shift regarding the way in which assistance is provided' (ec.europa.eu). Indeed, JESSICA is a mechanism that deviates from the logic of grants directed to cities through managing authorities of the public sector and seeks to take advantage of financial engineering. Financial mechanisms, like loans, are used with a view to producing revenue that can then be reinvested on urban projects. JESSICA seeks to mobilize private capital investment on urban development encouraging Public Private Partnerships (PPPs). Local authorities need to form partnerships with banks or other private investors on projects and ensure that there will be low risk and enhanced return for the private investor in the long run. This, in turn, will ensure long term financing of urban development projects. Projects funded by JESSICA can be either urban regeneration or energy focused. They have to be part of an urban strategy and can be either area or city based.[2]

A shift can be observed from a period when urban interventions were expected to boost the local economy and urban competitiveness to the global economy to a new era where urban interventions are themselves expected to produce revenue and funds for more projects. This shift is facilitated by a significant shift in terms of governance. The private sector enters the scene as a key stakeholder of urban regeneration. Horizontal networks of national and sub-national authorities, private actors and banks have to be forged, rather than vertical hierarchies. Networks are initiated and funds are managed directly by municipalities and not by the regional authorities, as were the ERDF funds. JESSICA is negotiated between prospective partners, circumventing intermediate levels of governance. Europeanization requires a new paradigm shift that reduces public authorities to mere stakeholders.

Thessaloniki, as mentioned above, does not have an updated strategic plan and the *Organization* overviewing urban projects at a metropolitan level was abolished in 2014. The Municipality of Thessaloniki was the first local authority in Greece to actually engage in a PPP with Piraeus Bank to activate JESSICA for an urban development project. The two partners signed an agreement in May 2016, securing funding through an Urban Development Fund (UDF) created by JESSICA, for a city-wide project of urban infrastructure. Replacing street lighting with energy efficient led lamps, the project had a strong energy focus contributing to the city's transition to a more sustainable use of energy. It is estimated that the new lamps will save 67% of energy required for lighting and will improve levels of visual comfort in the streets (www.thessaloniki.gr).

Environmental sustainability is equated to energy efficiency. Embracing the latest European terminology, innovative technology is employed towards reducing, in a quantifiable manner, the impact of the city on the planet and mitigating climate change. Nature in this case is identified with the planetary ecosystem that human activity is depleting and degrading. As funding through the UDF is hoped to recycle funds, the project aims to be financially sustainable and produce more funds for future urban interventions. Nevertheless, social sustainability, the third dimension of sustainable development, is out of the picture. The projected percentage of energy reduction for lighting, as the sole expected environmental outcome of the intervention is a testimony to a narrowing conceptualization of sustainability, as it is construed in EU policy documents and transferred through novel funding mechanisms.

Concluding remarks

Greece's national planning legislation embraced sustainability and urban regeneration during the 1990s. Mainstream imaginaries of sustainability, as developed gradually in successive EU documents, were reflected in Greek planning laws transferring first the holistic nature of the concept, and later its relationship to market economy and urban competitiveness. The compact city model was endorsed, as a sustainable urban form, despiteits limited relevance to the Greek urban context. However, the planning system retained its rigidity and remained incongruent to developments in EU spatial policy initiatives. Starting at 2010, the financial crisis functioned as a great thrust of change for the national planning framework, dismantling previous stages and bodies of planning, and introducing strategic spatial planning and the tools to implement it. Sustainability remained the predominant theme. Resilience, however, did not enter the national planning system, nor did the need to adapt climate change. The imaginary of the city as resilient, adaptive to planetary risks, attractive and competitive, prevalent in EU documents, was spurred in the context of the crisis through urban initiatives and projects, which were not necessarily linked to the planning system, its vertical tiers and its institutions.

Left in a limbo state, due to shrinkage of state funding and no up-to-date strategic plan at a metropolitan level, Thessaloniki developed a sustainability agenda, performing a unique trajectory across levels of governance, and not through the hierarchies of instituted tiers of formal planning. Endorsing EU's changing imaginaries and adapting to EU processes, the city promoted its urban regeneration objectives in a period of crisis. The Municipality of Thessaloniki has been increasingly active in 'downloading' (Marshall 2005) European imaginaries, policies and governance reforms with a view to securing large quantities of European funding. Materialising the urge of EU urban policy to connect with other cities to exchange 'best practices', Thessaloniki's projects were also 'uploaded' into European internet platforms. Thus, they are recognized as 'best practices' and potentially as shapers of EU's future policies with regard to sustainable urban regeneration. Most importantly, they project the city's newly forged green identity to the world.

The paper discussed EU funded projects in Thessaloniki along two axes. Along the first axis, the paper traced changing imaginaries of sustainability, following closely equivalent shifts in EU policy priorities. EU funded urban interventions in Thessaloniki as first introduced in the 1990s centred around the promotion of the city's historic character, as well as the improvement of social amenities in under-privileged parts of the city.

Sustainability first became a priority of urban regeneration projects during the 2000s. Urban projects with a clearly stated environmental agenda have become the norm in a context of austerity politics. As state funding shrunk, the central municipality 'europeanised' its priorities, placing sustainability at the centre of its policy agenda.EU discursive shifts, as discussed earlier in this paper, have been assimilated accordingly. The paper unveiled prevailing imaginaries of nature and the environment as they filtered in Thessaloniki's projects from EU policy documents. Notwithstanding the overarching nature of sustainability, as originally defined by the Brundtland Report and gradually endorsed by EU policy documents, and its recent conspicuous enhancement with the urgent imperative of resilience, the paper outlines a constantly narrowing conceptualization of sustainability in projects in Thessaloniki. Nature, traditionally seen as separate from society, has increasingly been identified with specific aspects of the environment. Urban sustainability, as shown in the refashioning of the New Waterfront, was identified with increased greenery, reflecting the original imaginary of 'nature in the city' as promoted in the *Green Paper* of 1990. In subsequent projects, it was identified with 'innovative' technical fixes vindicated on the grounds of measurable outcomes, like reductions in temperature or CO_2 emissions. This trend goes hand in hand with the imperative for urban interventions to contribute to urban competitiveness and produce revenue. Networks and information exchange also became a prominent goal, as reflected in

Table 1. Levels of governance, EU funding mechanisms and imaginaries of sustainability in Thessaloniki projects.

	Levels of governance	EU funding mechanism	Type of project	Sustainability imaginary
1991–1996 'Urban Pilot Project for Renewal and Development of the Historic Commercial centre of Thessaloniki'	National regional Metropolitan municipal	Urban pilot project – ERDF	Area-based	no
1994–1999 Interventions at the Western districts of Thessaloniki	national regional Metropolitan municipal	URBAN Community Initiative (URBAN I)	Area-based	no
1996 Thessaloniki Cultural Capital of Europe	national regional metropolitan municipal	European Capital of Europe	Area-based	no
2006–2014 Redesigning the New Waterfront of Thessaloniki	regional metropolitan municipal	ERDF – Axis: environment	Area-based	Increased urban greenery
2014–2016 Climatic Upgrade of Chrimatistiriou Square district	Regional municipal	ERDF – Axis: environment – sustainable development	Area-based	Reduced CO_2 emissions Reduced urban temperatures Energy efficiency Adaptation to climate change
2016 Promoting cycling	municipal	URBACT III Resilient Europe	Area-based Network building	Resilience Promotion of cycling Networking Citizen participation
2016 Replacing street lighting	municipal	JESSICA	Target – based Fund recycling	Energy efficiency Mitigation of climate change Financial sustainability

the city's participation in an URBACT III project as well as in many European and international networks in the 2010s. Finally, in the recent intervention through JESSICA, sustainability came to be synonymous to financial sustainability (Table 1).

Centering around narrowing environmental objectives, recent projects sidelined wider issues of urban development. Major regeneration projects started in the 1990s as area – based, addressing a variety of issues within the designated areas, ranging from traffic infrastructure to institutional changes, to become in recent years target-based, targeting single issues and specific measurable outcomes, like reduction of energy used for street lighting or promoting cycling. While economic sustainability increased its share in recent agendas, social sustainability, as a goal of urban regeneration, became marginalized, and the original holistic nature of the concept became compromised.

The second axis discussed changing processes through which sustainability was transferred in Thessaloniki's projects. The three projects that were implemented during the 1990s, before the introduction of sustainability in the city's agenda, involved all levels of governance, national regional and local and were supervised by the metropolitan planning authority which sought to guarantee adherence to the city's strategic plan of 1985. However, austerity politics left the metropolitan area of Thessaloniki without a binding comprehensive and up-to-date strategy and with no metropolitan planning authority. Recent urban projects towards sustainability adhere to a strategy created, not as part of institutionalized processes of the planning system, but as a result of the city's participation to an international network initiated and funded by a big philanthropic foundation.

Moreover, the recent troika-imposed 'planning reform' introduced a strategic dimension to the national planning system. Presumably, this alleviates the previous 'institutional misfit' between a rigid planning system of the South European 'urbanism tradition' and the flexible strategic character of the EU spatial policy. While domestic planning frameworks were being reworked at a national level, EU funding was successfully claimed and urban regeneration projects were planned and implemented in Thessaloniki. This may be interpreted as a local reflection of the relativisation of existing spatial hierarchies in EU planning systems and the foregrounding of the metropolitan level as a pivotal sub-national scale (Reimer, Getimis, and Blotevogel 2014, 14). New EU processes and funding mechanisms, addressed specifically to cities and managed by cities, i.e. JESSICA, relativized, if not altogether deconstructed, established hierarchies within the domestic planning system, introduced new actors and facilitated the creation of ad hoc horizontal networks. The crisis has acted as a catalyst in this process. In a context of reduced state funding and planning vagueness, Thessaloniki adapted its governance to secure much needed funding for urban interventions.

In conclusion, sustainability has been transferred in Thessaloniki in changing conceptualizations and through different processes. The recent shift to climate adaptation and resilience, in terms of imaginaries pursued, and the 'turn to strategy' (Reimer et al., 13) in terms of planning processes, are responses to a changing financial and institutional environment constituted in multiple scales, from the global to the urban. Both changes may be interpreted as signs of increased 'Europeanisation' of Thessaloniki's urban policies. They are not however a one-way adaptive process descending geographical scales, but a complex and dialectic trajectory.

Notes

1. The network was started in 2008 with 'the ambition to gather local governments voluntarily committed to achieving and exceeding the EU climate and energy targets' (https://www.covenantofmayors.eu). The municipality of Thessaloniki has joined the network in 2011 and presented an action plan to reduce energy consumption.
2. However, Nadler and Nadler (2018), assessing the 55 projects funded through JESSICA in its first programming period (2007–2013), discovered that many of them were regional and not urban projects.

Acknowledgements

The author would like to thank Dr Maria Karagianni and Dr MatinaKapsali for their help with the drafting of Diagram 1.

Disclosure statement

No potential conflict of interest was reported by the author.

References

Andreou, G. 2006. "EU Cohesion Policy in Greece: Patterns of Governance and Europeanization." *South European Society & Politics* 11 (2): 241–259. doi:10.1080/13608740600645865.

Athanassiou, E. 2000. "European Sustainable Cities: Common Goals for Different Contexts", 5th International Conference on the Protection and Restoration of the Environment, Conference Proceeding, 1147–1154. Thassos, 3–6 July.

Athanassiou, E. 2015. "Green Urban Strategies in Thessaloniki in the Context of Crisis." In *Keeping up with Technologies to Improve Places*, edited by E. VaništaLazarević, M. Vukmirović, A. Krstić-Furundžić, and A. Đukić, 178–188. Newcastle upon Tyne: Cambridge Scholar Publishing. ISBN-13: 978-1-4438-7739-8.

Brenner, N., and N. Theodore, eds. 2002. *Spaces of Neoliberalism: Urban Restructuring in North America and Western Europe*. Oxford: Blackwell.

Bulkeley, H., and M. Betsill. 2005. "Rethinking Sustainability: Multilevel Governance and the "Urban" Politics of Climate Change." *Environmental Politics* 14 (1): 42–63. doi:10.1080/09644010042000310178.

City of Thessaloniki. 2016. "Resilient Thessaloniki: A Strategy for 2030." 7 October 2019. https://thessaloniki.gr

Commission of the European Communities (CEC). 1990. "Green Paper of the Urban Environment." *COM(90) 218 final*. Brussels. https://publications.europa.eu

Deffner, A. M., and L. Labrianidis. 2005. "Planning Culture and Time in a Mega-event: Thessaloniki as the European City of Culture in 1997." *International Planning Studies*. Routledge, 10 (3–4): 241–264. doi:10.1080/13563470500378556.

EC. 2010. Making our cities attractive and sustainable: *How the EU contributes to improving the urban environment* Luxembourg: Publications Office of the European Union

EU. 2014. "URBACT III Operational Programme." January 2019. http://urbact.eu/sites/default/files/u_iii_op_adopted_12_december_2014.pdf

EU. 2016. "Urban Resilience: A Concept for Co-creating Cities for the Future." http://urbact.eu/sites/default/files/resilient_europe_baseline_study.pdf

EU & UN. 2016. "The State of European Cities 2016: Cities Leading the Way to a Better Future, Luxembourg: Publications Office of the European Union." 7 December 2018. https://ec.europa.eu/regional_policy/sources/docgener/informat/2014/guidance_sustainable_urban_development_en.pdf

European Commission (EC). 1996. "European Sustainable Cities." *Report, Expert group on the urban environment, Directorate General XI*. Brussels.

European Commission (EC). 1997. *The EU Compendium of Spatial Planning Systems and Policies*. Luxembourg: Official Publications of the European Communities.

European Commission (EC). 2013. "Living Well, within the Limits of Our Planet." 13 June 2018. https://eur-lex.europa.eu

European Commission (EC). 2016. "Guidance for Member States on Intergrated Sustainable Urban Development (Article 7 ERDF Regulation)."

Getimis, P., and G. Giannakourou. 2014. "The Evolution of Spatial Planning in Greece after the 1990s: Drivers, Directions and Agents of Change." In *Spatial Planning Systems and Practices in Europe: A Comparative Perspective on Continuity and Changes*, edited by M. Reimer, P. Getimis, and H. H. Blotevogel, 149–165. New York: Routledge.

Giannakourou, G. 2005. "Transforming Spatial Planning Policy in the Mediterranean Countries: Europeanization and Domestic Change." *European Planning Studies* 12 (2): 319–331. doi:10.1080/0365431042000321857.

Government Newsletter. 1997. "Sustainable Development of Cities and Settlements (124 A 13/6/1997)."

Government Newsletter. 1999. "Spatial Planning and Sustainable Development (207 A 7/10/1999)."

Government Newsletter. 2015. "Project of Integrated Urban Intervention for the Centre of Athens (No 64, Vol.2)."

Harvey, D. 2006. *Spaces of Global Capitalism Towards a Theory of Uneven Geographical Development*. London: Verso.

Hastaoglou-Martinidis, V., N. Kalogirou, and N. Papamichos. 1993. "The Revaluing of Urban Space: The Green Paper for European Cities and the Case of Greece." *Antipode* 25 (3): 240–252. doi:10.1111/j.1467-8330.1993.tb00457.x.

http://nws.eurocities.eu/MediaShell/media/CoM_Thessaloniki_EL.pdf

Karadimitriou, N., and T. Pagonis. 2019. "Planning Reform Anddevelopment Rights in Greece: Institutional Persistence and Elite Rule in the Face of the Crisis." *European Planning Studies* 27: 1217–1234. doi:10.1080/09654313.2019.1579300.

Marshall, A. 2005. "Europeanization at the Urban Level: Local Actors, institutions and the Dynamics of Multi-level Interaction." *Journal of European Public Policy* 12 (4): 668–686. doi:10.1080/13501760500160292.

Meadows, D. H., D. L. Meadows, J. Randers, and W. W. Behrens. 1972. *The Limits to Growth*. London: Potomac Associates.

Medeiros, E. A., and A. Van der Zwet. 2019. "Evaluating Integrated Sustainable Urban Development Strategies: A Methodological Framework Applied in Portugal." *European Planning Studies*. doi:10.1080/09654313.2019.1606898.

Mol, A. P. J., D. A. Sonnerfeld, and G. Spaargaren, eds. 2009. *The Ecological Modernisation Reader. Environmental Reform in Theory and Practice*. London/New York: Routledge.

Municipality of Thessaloniki. (2018). Integrated Action Plan for Urban Resilience through promoting cycling policies and culture throughout Thessaloniki, Sustainable Mobility and Networks Directorate, Transport Planning Department. Retrieved from https://thessaloniki.gr 20 June 2020

Nadler M. and Nadler C. (2018) Promoting investment in sustainable urban development with JESSICA: Outcomes of a new EU policy initiative, 55:9, pp. 1839–1858. doi:10.1177/0042098017702815.

NSRF. 2014–2020. Accessed 24 January 2019. https://www.espa.gr

Official Journal of the EU. (2006). Thematic strategy for the urban environment, C 306 E 15 December 2006, pp. 182–188. Retrieved from https://eur-lex.europa.eu/resource.html?uri=cellar:9935b309-54b0-4793-8a4d-6af745b48009.0005.02/DOC_84&format=PDF 20 June 2020

Papadopoulos, L., ed. 2001. *Transformations of the Urban Landscape: Schemes and Projects of the Organisation of Cultural Capital of Europe Thessaloniki 1997*. Thessaloniki: LivanisNeaSinora.

Reimer, M., P. Getimis, and H. H. Blotevogel. 2014. "Spatial Planning Systems and Practices in Europe: A Comparative Perspective." In *Spatial Planning Systems and Practices in Europe: A Comparative Perspective on Continuity and Changes*, edited by M. Reimer, P. Getimis, and H. H. Blotevogel, 1–20. New York: Routledge.

Smith, N. 1984. Uneven development: Nature capital and the production of space, In *Athens Georgia*: Georgia University Press

Smith, N. 2006. "Foreward." In *In the Nature of Cities: Urban Political Ecology and the Politics of Urban Metabolism*, edited by N. Heynen, M. Kaika, and E. Swyngedouw, 1–20. New York: Routledge.

URBACT. 2017. "The URBACT III Programme Manual." Accessed 7 December 2018. http://urbact.eu/sites/default/files/programme_manual_v8_after_nov_2017_mc_meeting.pdf

Urban Pilot Project. Accessed 24 January 2019. https://ec.europa.eu/regional_policy/archive/urban2/urban/upp/src/bullet07.htm#thei Accessed 20 June 2020.

Vitopoulou, A., and A. Yiannakou. 2018. "Public Land Policy and Urban Planning in Greece: Diachronic Continuities and Abrupt Reversals in a Context of Crisis." *European Urban and Regional Studies*. doi:10.1177/0969776418811894.

World Commission on Environment and Development (WCED). 1987. *Our Common Future*. Oxford: Oxford University Press.

Understanding the influence of EU urban policy in Spanish cities: the case of Málaga

Sonia De Gregorio Hurtado

ABSTRACT
This work aims to shed light on the contribution of the urban dimension of the Cohesion Policy (CP) to Spanish cities. It is based on the case study of Málaga, a city in which European Union (EU) programmes have contributed importantly to regenerating its historic centre. The case study uses a mixed qualitative methodology to understand if and to what extent the EU urban programmes have delivered local capacity. The results show that their contribution has been positive, but also identifies the persistence of inertia and relevant contradictions that provide lessons for the post-2020 urban dimension of the CP.

1. Introduction

During the last three decades, the European Union (EU) has supported cities in tackling urban decline through explicit initiatives and programmes. Following the initial experience of the Urban Pilot Projects (UPP) of 1989, in 1994 the European Commission launched the URBAN Community Initiative, an instrument that started to shape the essence of EU policy approach to sustainable urban development. In a period characterized by political, economic and spatial transformation (Hall 1987; Campos Venuti 1987), the European Economic Community (EEC) started to pay attention to the urban issue with the objective of regenerating deprived urban neighbourhoods. URBAN (1994–1999) and its second round, URBAN II (2000–2007), implemented urban regeneration programmes in around 200 cities across Europe, putting into place methodological elements such as the cross-sectoral coordination of actions (integrated approach), strong horizontal partnerships, and the concentration of funding in selected vulnerable target areas (the area-based approach) (European Commission 2008; De Gregorio Hurtado 2012). The literature shows that, while '*URBAN-style area-based initiatives were already taking place in some member-states* (e.g. the UK and France), *in the majority of countries the URBAN Community Initiative presented an innovative way of addressing area-based urban challenges, effectively leading the way for a sea-change in thinking on urban regeneration in many member-states, both in terms of content and process*' (Carpenter, 2006: 2145).

The policy action of the ECC was contextualized in an international framework in which many socio-economic, cultural and institutional trends of change converged, giving way to a new generation of public policies (Romero 2005, 63), from amongst which urban regeneration emerged. This policy domain was a result of the evolution of the urban policy initiatives developed in some countries during the 1970s and the 1980s, in which the role of partnerships gradually gained visibility and relevance, and a more consensual style of politics was embedded (Roberts & Sykes, 2000) in the framework of a change that has been conceptualized as the 'communicative turn' (Healey, 1997). This was complemented by the recognition of a series of new problems and challenges in the 1990s (Roberts & Sykes, 2000), in particular, environmental problems and the issue of sustainability, that started to be addressed through the so-called integrated approach to overcoming the sectoral visions that characterized the urban renewal. The Rio Summit of United Nations and the resulting Rio Declaration gave visibility to these issues in 1992 at an international level. In 1994, this attention was reinforced in the European framework by the Aalborg Charter. At the time, all these elements shaped the emerging urban dimension of the ECC policy to support cities in facing urban decline and were also embedded in the policy documents produced.

Together with URBAN and URBAN II, throughout the 1994–2016 period, the development of policy documents was crucial for the 'formalization' of what we today can call the urban policy of the EU. They have been produced by different actors, among which are the European Commission, a number of EU Presidencies (Atkinson and Walliser 2013), other EU bodies (e.g. the European Parliament, the Committee of the Regions, etc.), and external organizations, such as Eurocities (De Gregorio Hurtado 2012). The instruments and documents mentioned have been significantly complemented by other initiatives launched by the European Commission at different moments (e.g. the URBACT programme in 2000). All these developments have laid the base for a common EU approach to address urban development (De Gregorio Hurtado 2012) in the member-states, resulting in the so-called Urban Acquis of the EU (European Commission 2009).

The genealogy and results of the influence that the urban policy of the EU has exerted in the different countries have been widely addressed and analysed by the literature on the urban dimension of Europeanization (see for example: Dukes 2008; Cotella and Janin Rivolin 2011; De Gregorio Hurtado 2012; Carpenter 2013; Adshead 2014; Tortola 2016). It has demonstrated how the role played by the UE institutions in this regard has resulted in a complex interactive framework in which the UE and member states have exerted mutual influence, giving place to relevant progress, but also showing how the introduction of innovation in domestic frameworks has been limited in many cases by path dependence and policy inertias that have hindered the construction of local capacity. Over time, this policy has been formalized as a soft policy (thus not statutory), that needs to be flexible in order to be adapted to many different national contexts. The role of 'gatekeeper' played by the member states (Tofarides 2003) has also conditioned the results achieved.

In Spain, the literature has shown that the contribution of the policy interaction mentioned has exerted an important influence on the different levels of government with competences on urban matters (De Gregorio Hurtado 2012, 2014, 2017a). This can be explained because the country has never developed a distinct national urban policy (Parkinson, De Gregorio Hurtado, and Lefèvre 2013; Del Castillo and Haarich 2013) and because of the 'passive' role it has played in the framework of the interaction described, which has identified it as a policy-taker from an Europeanization perspective (González Medina et al. 2017).

In this framework, the EU contribution has allowed many Spanish cities to familiarise themselves with the model of sustainable urban development encoded in the Urban Acquis and the method for urban regeneration (the URBAN method) proposed by the UE (De Gregorio Hurtado 2017b), as well as to get funding to implement it. Because of this, it can be considered that today the discourse on sustainable urban development and urban regeneration embedded in the EU urban policy documents and instruments has been transferred to the discourse on urban sustainability of the majority of the Spanish cities (De Gregorio Hurtado 2018). Some of them have been able to use the knowledge and experience gained through their participation in the mentioned programmes to build local capacity and to put collaborative governance models into place, even if it has been observed that they find relevant limitations when attempting to root these elements in their technical and administrative practices (ibid.). In any case, the capacity developed by cities is considered a relevant result of the EU programmes. This is because if it is embedded in the 'common' practice of the municipalities, it can be replicated once the programmes are finished, providing an added value that can result in transformative practices, and thus in the further construction of local capacity.

This paper aims to contribute to the reflection on the Europeanization of urban local policies focusing on the Spanish scenario with the objective of shedding light on what has been the effect of the urban dimension of the Cohesion Policy at the muncipal level, and particularly in the cities that appear in the collective imagination to be more proactive and capable of developing local capacity through the implementation of specific urban programmes. In order to address this objective, the paper focuses on the case study of the city of Málaga. It has been selected amongst many other Spanish cities as it is considered by practitioners, academics, policy-makers, and public servants to be a representative example of a city that has significantly built on the urban dimension of Cohesion Policy to transform its historic centre (see Part 3).

The analysis follows this structure: Section 2 presents the framework of urban regeneration in the country, introducing the contribution of the urban dimension of Cohesion Policy and explaining how in the Spanish case it has been instrumental in creating a meaningful link between the local and the EU level. Section 3 introduces the analytical framework, the materials and methods, and the case study of Málaga. Section 4 presents Málaga and contextualizes the situation of the decline of the historic city centre at the beginning of the 1990s. Section 5 focuses on the specific programmes through which the urban dimension of Cohesion Policy has contributed to the regeneration of the city centre (URBAN (1994–1999), Iniciativa Urbana (2007–2013), and EDUSI (2014–2020)). Section 6 presents the conclusions and a series of recommendations for the post-2020 period of the Cohesion Policy.

2. Urban regeneration in Spain: main issues from the beginning of the Democratic Period (1975) to the present

As it has been pointed out, Spain is one of the member states of the EU that has not developed an explicit urban policy (Parkinson, De Gregorio Hurtado, and Lefèvre

2013). This is explained by a relevant number of factors that are interrelated and deeply rooted in the tradition of urban policies inherited from the past. Among these, in the framework of this article, it is necessary to mention the following: i) the traditional non-collaborative governance style in policy-making; ii) the way in which the institutional and policy framework on urban issues was shaped, based on the Constitution of 1978, and its evolution from that moment to present day. Regarding the first, Romero (2005) argues that in Spain the tradition of sectoral planning and an insufficient political culture in the domains of institutional coordination and territorial cooperation prevails. This scenario is complemented by a lack of tradition of participation in the public domain that particularly affects urban policies (see for example: Urrutia 1992; Borja 2002). The second factor mentioned has resulted in most of the competences on urban policies (that were previously centralized) being devolved to the regions (Autonomous Communities) and the municipalities.

In this general framework, the Spanish Government has not developed specific legislative or funding frameworks to support cities in the regeneration of their vulnerable urban areas, which contrasts with the relevance that the issue gained in the late 1990s in the context of the EU as an increasingly strategic policy field for national socio-economic development. It also contrasts with the policy attention paid to this topic by other member states of the EU, which resulted in many of them launching policy schemes for urban regeneration at a national level. Some of these countries have developed specific initiatives[1] following the reference of the URBAN Community Initiative. Interestingly, in Spain, the only initiatives that have addressed this policy issue at a national scale have been the instruments launched in the framework of the urban dimension of the Cohesion Policy. Because of this, these Initiatives have exerted a very important influence on cities and the general urban policy framework of the country (De Gregorio Hurtado, 2012; De Gregorio Hurtado, 2017a, 2018).

As mentioned above, the Autonomous Communities have competences regarding many urban policy issues, including urban regeneration. This level of government did not act on this point until the first half of the 2000s. During that decade three regions launched instruments for urban regeneration directly inspired by URBAN: In 2004, Catalonia passed the so-called 'Ley de Barrios' (*Neighbourhoods Law*). In 2009, a similar law was passed in the Balearic Islands, but a lack of continuity in the provision of funds rendered it ineffective. URBAN also influenced the IZARTU programme (De Gregorio Hurtado, 2012) for urban regeneration, launched in the Basque Country in 2001. During the 2000s other Autonomous Communities also planned to develop regeneration initiatives, but the arrival of the economic crisis in 2007 put an end to them before they could be formalized (Ibíd.). At the moment, some regions are moving ahead again (e.g. in 2018 the Basque Country launched an initiative for the regeneration of the most vulnerable urban areas, the initiative Repensar los Barrios I + D + I – Rethink the Neighbourhoods R + D + I-).

In this general framework, the lack of specific support from the upper levels of government for the regeneration of deprived urban neighbourhoods has fostered the 'link' between Spanish cities and the EU. The first have found in the second, interesting realistic possibilities to secure funding and access to guidelines on how to address sustainable urban development and integrated urban regeneration. '*In a context of regional and Central Government inertia, the EU has provided a model and guidance for sustainable urban development and urban regeneration in Spanish cities for the past two decades*' (De Gregorio Hurtado, 2017a: 403). This situation has resulted in a sort of 'channel' through which cities have been able to achieve a direct relation with the EU bodies that launch or manage urban programmes. This has been a relevant driver of Europeanization in the country and the one that has resulted in Spanish cities being particularly active in the framework of EU urban programmes in which the calls are directly launched at an EU level without the intermediary role of the member states (e.g. URBACT and the Urban Innovative Actions).

3. Analytical framework, materials and methods

3.1 *Analytical framework*

To develop the case study of Málaga, this article has started off from the study of the EU documents related to sustainable urban development, in the framework of the analysis undertaken by the author on the implementation of the urban dimension of Cohesion Policy in Spain from 1994 until today (De Gregorio Hurtado, 2012, 2017a, 2018). The documents are European Commission communications that set the base for the development of the urban instruments funded by the Cohesion Policy in each programming period, as well as documents that have contributed to the Urban Acquis of the EU. These documents clearly explain the method for integrated urban regeneration proposed by the EU over time, and their revision allows us to identify their main innovative methodological elements: the integrated approach and the adoption of the partnership principle in urban regeneration programmes. Taking into account that the aim of this paper is to understand the contribution of the urban instruments of the Cohesion Policy implemented in Spain in the creation of local capacity in Málaga, the study adopts a temporal perspective aimed at understanding if the development of the earlier instruments has given place to experience and knowledge in the following instruments, producing local capacity. In order to make this analysis possible, and building on the review of the policy documents and the literature, the study proposes two analytical categories that permit the operationalization of the investigation of the different instruments developed in Málaga. They are the following:

(i) The level of adoption of the integrated approach to urban development (understood as cross-sectoral coordination of actions (European Commission 2008)) in the strategies for urban regeneration. To analyse this issue, the study focuses on the kind of measures integrated into the urban regeneration strategies of the instruments studied. The aim is to understand whether all the relevant dimensions of urban decline were addressed in a balanced way. The analysis also addresses the level of 'coherence' in the implementation of the integrated approach, directed at understanding if there were clear and justified interrelations among the different measures foreseen by the strategy, and the capacity of these interrelations to yield synergies capable of reinforcing the overall proposal.

(ii) The embeddedness of collaborative governance models, focusing on the participation of actors of the local community through the implementation of the partnership principle. To analyse this issue, the study focuses on the governance model defined in the strategies for urban regeneration analysed and, in particular, in the provision (or not) of clear frameworks for public participation and the economic resources necessary. The analysis addresses the governance model in two different stages: 1) the definition of the strategy, and 2) the implementation of the strategy.

The two analytical categories are addressed through a mixed qualitative method based on the analysis of primary sources (particularly the documents developed in the context of the programmes analysed) and literature. When the analysis of these sources has not provided information regarding specific issues, interviews have been conducted with key stakeholders in the Municipality of Málaga and the Ministry that manages the urban instruments funded by the Cohesion Policy in Spain (see acknowledgements).

3.2 *Justification of the case study: Malaga*

The analysis of the implementation of the urban dimension of EU policy in Spain over time allows us to recognise that some cities were pioneers in understanding the relevant opportunities that could come from the EU level and the funding available to cope with urban decline at the beginning of the 1990s. Because of this, in the first half of that decade they created their departments of European projects, aimed at developing the necessary skills to get EU funding to regenerate their deprived neighbourhoods and to address sectoral issues focusing on the identification of funding schemes. In this framework, Málaga arises as one of the first Spanish cities that created a Department of European Projects (in 1993).

As mentioned, Málaga has been a particularly active city in the field of urban policy, developing an activity that has been prominently disseminated by the Municipality. It was the first Andalusian city to undertake its Strategic Plan (1992) and one of the first in Spain. It was also one of the first cities that approved its Local Agenda 21 (1995) in the country. This Agenda has been continuously updated by the Municipality, and in 2015 it was converted into the urban agenda for the city, anticipating the framework that many cities are developing in the framework of the Agenda 2030 for Sustainable Development (2015) and the Sustainable Development Goals -SDGs- (Armondi and De Gregorio Hurtado, 2019). The sustained agenda-process undertaken by Málaga throughout the last decades has established a well-founded framework that allows the city to monitor its dynamics and the effect produced by the policies implemented (on the basis of a solid set of indicators).

Beyond all this, the case of Málaga emerges as particularly interesting in making a contribution to the reflection on the effects of the urban dimension of the Cohesion Policy in Spain in terms of capacity building. This is because it has been one of the few cities that have developed specific urban instruments in three out of the four of the last programming periods of the Cohesion Policy funded by the European Regional Development Fund (ERDF) and the European Social Fund (ESF). The positive influence of these instruments in the city has been recognized. It has been argued that the '*great majority of the programmes and actions undertaken for the regeneration of the historic centre, have been developed with the support of EU Funds, in particular the URBAN Community Initiative, the Iniciativa Urbana, other ERDF Funds, Interreg, etc.*' (Barreiro 2013, 11). The Municipality recognizes this ('*The Municipality of Málaga initiated with the URBAN Community Initiative in 1995 a process of recuperation of the historic centre (...)'* (Ayuntamiento de Málaga, undated: 1)).

Moreover, it is recognized that the development of these programmes of urban regeneration has given place to a learning process in the city, entailing the construction of local capacity (interview 1) that has been embedded in the development and implementation of the more recent instruments. For this reason, this analysis adopts a chronological approach that aims to understand whether there has been a positive evolution over time regarding the analytical categories proposed to develop the study.

4. Presentation of the case study: Málaga

Málaga is located in the region of Andalusia, in the coastal area of the Mediterranean Sea called the Costa del Sol (see Figure 1). In 2017, it reached a population of 570.000 inhabitants. It is the second most populous city of the region and the sixth of the country.

As in most of the large and medium-sized Spanish cities, the population has increased dramatically since the 1940s. The new inhabitants settled in the outskirts, in self-constructed substandard housing, or in the city centre, where a process of overcrowding and decay took place. During the 1950s, Málaga´s urban plan ried to address this situation through new planned developments (mainly promoted by the State) and by providing the lacking facilities and infrastructures. This applied until the mid-1960s. From this point onwards, Málaga underwent a process of extraordinary growth due to the development of the tourism sector and the fact that, to boost economic development, the so-called National Plans for Development (*Planes Nacionales de Desarrollo*) prevailed over the urban plans developed by the State. The result in Málaga was that the real estate sector took over the initiative for the new expansion development. In the 1960–1981 period, the population increased from around

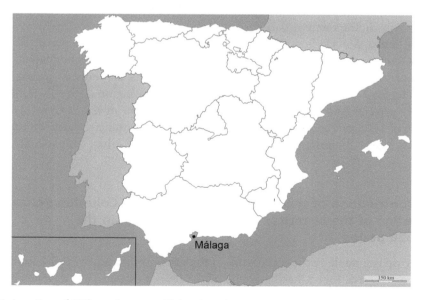

Figure 1. Location of Málaga. Source: self-developed.

300,000 to approximately 500,000 inhabitants, something that contrasts with the trend shown by most populous Spanish cities, in which from the second half of the 1970s the population started to stabilize or even to shrink (Sainz Gutiérrez 2006). This fact resulted in new urban areas characterized by a low level of planning control, the accelerated construction of residential buildings, and the lack of services and facilities, being poorly connected with other parts of the city. At the same time, the old city centre continued experiencing a process of decline fostered by the demolition of some areas in which new residential buildings were to be constructed. In 1983, a new urban plan was established. It was based on a different understanding of urban development and prioritised finishing with the uncontrolled growth of the 1970s and the first 1980s and the revitalization of the old city centre. Continuing in this vein, in 1988 the Plan of Protection of the old city centre (*Plan Especial de Protección y Reforma Interior – PEPRI*) was passed. The PEPRI established the rules for the renovation and construction of new buildings with the goal of maintaining and protecting the traditional character and value of the centre. Afterwards, the main objectives of the 1983 Plan were integrated in the new 1996 urban plan. The revitalization of the old city centre continued to be a priority. This period of rationalization of urban growth ended during the real state bubble of the 1990s and the early 2000s, in which all the Spanish urban areas, and particularly the most dynamic metropoles as well as those located on the Mediterranean Coast, underwent a significant growth. The consequence in Málaga was that one-fourth of the existing buildings in 2010 had been constructed in the 2000–2010 period (Ferrary 2010). Even if this trend was present in all the large- and medium-sized cities in the country, Málaga was the second city in terms of growth during that period (ibid.). It is also worth noting that at present, the 'regenerated' historical city centre is undergoing a strong touristification trend (Marín, Guevara, and Navarro-Jurado 2017). The city centre of Malaga has undergone an urban regeneration process through three different specific urban instruments launched in the framework of the Cohesion Policy of the EU from 1994, which will be further explained in this paper. It is important to take this issue into account, as it can lead to a pertinent reflection on what the outcomes of the urban regeneration models that have been put into place during the last 30 years in the framework of the urban dimension of EU policy are.

As mentioned, Málaga is at the moment one of the Spanish cities perceived as being more pro-active in the field of urban sustainability in the country. This reputation contrasts with the touristification processes and other urban dynamics mentioned, and started to be cultivated by the Municipality at the end of the 1990s, drawing on i) the integration of the city in EU projects and programmes; ii) the dissemination of this activity. Today this perception of Málaga is consolidated. It has been reinforced and circulated widely because the city has received international recognition in the field of urban sustainability.

5. The contribution of the urban dimension of the Cohesion Policy in the regeneration of the historical city centre of Málaga in the 1994–2020 period

Málaga's case is notable in the framework of the urban dimension of Cohesion Policy in Spain. The reason is that it has been one of the few cities that have developed specific urban instruments during the course of three out of the last four programming periods of the Cohesion Policy. The instruments are as follows:

- URBAN Community Initiative (1994–1999)
- Iniciativa Urbana (IU) (2007–2013)
- Integrated Sustainable Urban Development Strategies – ISUDS – (*Estrategias de Desarrollo Sostenible Integrado – EDUSI*) (2014–2020).

Spain has been the only member state of the EU that has developed specific instruments for urban regeneration in the framework of the Cohesion Policy in the last four periods of the Cohesion Policy (De Gregorio Hurtado 2018). In this context, Málaga has implemented an URBAN programme (1994–1999), a programme under the Iniciativa Urbana (2000–2006), and is currently implementing an EDUSI (2014–2020). Other Spanish cities that have developed three of these instruments are Albacete, Córdoba, Sevilla, Santa Coloma de Gramanet and Palma de Mallorca (De Gregorio Hurtado 2017b). However, Málaga is the only case in which these instruments have applied in the same area of the city with an area-based approach.

5.1. *The URBAN programme in Málaga (1994–1999)*

Along with the expansion of the city, in the 1960s the historical centre of Malaga started to undergo a process of decline that resulted in a loss of population from the 1970s onwards and in its marginalization and deterioration (Ertan and Eercioglu 2016). At the beginning of the 1990s, it was the most deprived area of the city (Barreiro 2013). Even if some of the plans mentioned above considered this situation as a priority to be addressed, the efforts made during the 1980s were not sufficient to tackle the negative dynamics that were keeping the quality of life in the centre below average. The main limitations were related to the sizable extension of the city centre (40 hectares), the level of decay of the urban fabric and the public space, and the level of social vulnerability. To tackle this problem, the financial capacity of the Municipality was not sufficient (ibid.). In this context, Málaga looked to the EU as a support from which it was possible to get financial backing. At that moment, the European Commission was working on the definition of a new Community Initiative for the regeneration of deprived urban areas that in the end was titled URBAN and was launched through a call to the member states in July of 1994 (European Commission 1994). The call established and explained the 'method' that cities had to adopt to develop the URBAN programmes.

In Spain, cities accessed The URBAN Community Initiative (URBAN) by entering a competitive call launched by the Ministry of Finance (the institution responsible for the management of the European Regional Development Fund). The country was allocated ERDF and European Social Fund (ESF) resources to develop 29 URBAN programmes. In order to be selected, cities had to put into place an urban regeneration strategy for one of their most deprived areas, justify it and apply a method that introduced relevant innovative drivers, among others: i) the creation of partnerships in the framework of a participation process; ii) the integrated approach that implied addressing the social, economic, physical and environmental problems of the neighbourhoods through interrelated specific measures (De Gregorio Hurtado, 2012 and De Gregorio Hurtado 2014).

Málaga was one of the 29 Spanish cities selected to implement an URBAN programme. The experience and effort of the recently created Department of European

Figure 2. Area of development of the URBAN programme of Málaga. Source: self-developed on Google Maps following the explanations in (Barreiro, 2013: 21) in which it is mentioned that most of the measures of the URBAN programme were implemented within the area defined by the old city walls.

Projects were instrumental for the city to be able to produce a proposal that was admitted by the Initiative.

The URBAN programme of Málaga provided momentum to the transformation of the city centre (see Figure 2) under an integrated vision, focusing on the area inside the old city walls. In fact, it is acknowledged that the regeneration of the area started in 1994 with the support of 'European and municipal funds' (Barreiro 2013, 3). There, the URBAN programme concentrated political attention, and technical and economical efforts. The total amount that the programme devoted to the transformation of this area was 15,786,603 Euros (Barreiro 2013, 21).

5.1.1. *Addressing the integrated approach: measures integrated in the URBAN programme and their level of coherence*

As all the other Spanish URBAN programmes, the programme of Málaga was structured in a number of axes for action. Each of them integrated specific measures. Cities adapted this structure to their main problems by introducing measures only in those axes that were considered instrumental in addressing the decline of the selected area. In the case of Málaga, the specific actions were the following (see Table 1):

The specific actions proposed and developed focused mainly on the improvement of the urban environment (see Figure 3) and the investment in infrastructures, focusing

Table 1. Axes of action and measures implemented by the URBAN programme of Málaga. Source: self-developed, based on (Ministerio de Hacienda 2003a).

1. **Improvement of the urban environment**
   a. Aesthetical improvement of botanic itineraries.
   b. Signage of touristic itineraries.
   c. Refurbishment of degraded spaces.
   d. Park of Gibralfaro.
   e. Tunnel of Gibralfaro.
   f. Improvement of pavements, streets, urban furniture and lighting, and other urban infrastructures.
   g. Incentives for the rehabilitation of facades.
   h. Refurbishment of residual spaces.
2. **Development of the economic fabric**
   a. Improvement of commercial premises, modernization and provision of new furniture and internal installations.
   b. Collaboration with the Asociation Centro Historico Comercial to train and advise small traders.
3. **Social facilities**
   a. Improvement of the existing facilities for old people and provision of special vehicles for social services in the area of development of the URBAN programme.
   b. Center for the reception of visitors.
4. **Social services**
   a. Assistance of marginalized people through a mobile unit.
   b. Attention and social assistance through agreements signed with NGOs.
   c. Improvement of host community facilities
5. **Training programmes**
   a. Language training for the local police (French, English and German) to provide support to tourists.
6. **Monitoring, management, technical assistance, and evaluation.**
   a. Dissemination of the URBAN programme
      i. Audio-visual and didactic means to make aware children and young people of the urban challenges.
      ii. Itineraries in an 'environmental bus' with didactic, audio-visual, and working material on the environment.
      iii. Meetings with other cities developing URBAN programmes in Andalucía.
      iv. Creation of a web page for the URBAN programme of Malaga.

less attention on the social and economic domains. Regarding the last, the most important measure was the support of commercial activity.

The review of the measures integrated in the programme reveals that it was not addressing the main challenges of the city centre through specific innovative measures: the novelty introduced was mainly related to the implementation of the integrated approach, understood as the necessity to act in different dimensions of urban decline. This approach did not take into account the necessary coherence of the vision, which is a crucial element for creating synergy between the different measures proposed, deploying the added value of this holistic urban regeneration method. It is relevant to note, that with regard to the implementation of the integrated approach, the Municipality recognized that, for the city, the URBAN programme meant the introduction of a method based on integrated work that *'has remained over the years'* (Ayuntamiento de Málaga, undated: 1). The interview undertaken (interview 1. See acknowledgement) supports this statement, confirming that URBAN laid the foundations for the implementation of the integrated approach in future instruments.

5.1.2. *The governance model put into place to define and implement the regeneration strategy*

The URBAN method proposed another important innovation: it consisted in the creation of strong partnerships aimed at cultivating an agreed strategy of urban regeneration for a vulnerable area. In the case of Málaga, the programme concentrated the participation of the social actors focusing mainly on the traders' associations. This was justified because '*there were no representative groups of any other social sector*' (Prointec 2000, 17). The

Figure 3. Two streets of the elegible area of the URBAN programme before (left) and after (right) the implementation of the actions aimed to improve the urban environment (source: Barreiro, 2013: 23–24).

URBAN programme did not put into place any specific measure for participation, and the systems for the provision of information were based only on meetings to inform on some specific topics or to provide clarifications on them to local actors, the creation of a web page, and the dissemination in local media (ibid: 18). There were no arenas for debate that allowed the local community to present suggestions or demands (ibid.). This was one of the reasons why the population was uninformed in relation to the programme. In fact, the mid-term evaluation report mentioned that citizens did not relate the actions undertaken with URBAN and considered this a factor to be reviewed (ibid.: 38). The Municipality used the Strategic Plan of Málaga to identify the needs of the area. The Strategic Plan (1992–1995) was a participative instrument based on 40 meetings and the participation of approximately 2000 people in its preparation.

The limitation of the participation process in reference to the feedback received in the framework of the Strategic Plan meant that the city was only able to identify problems that were relevant to the historic city centre to a certain extent. The lack of a specific participation strategy minimized the potential of this kind of mechanism to create local capacity and a sense of co-responsibility in the non-institutional actors and citizens involved in the programme. It also limited the possibility of identifying specific resources not yet mobilized. The programme of Málaga was not an exception in the country. The lack of a participative tradition in urban regeneration limited the will and capacity of cities to put into place collaborative visions in the framework of the different URBAN programmes (De Gregorio Hurtado, 2012).

5.2. *The iniciativa urbana (IU) programme in Málaga (2007–2013)*

Before addressing the IU, it is worth remembering that during the 2000–2006 period Málaga did not implement a specific programme within the urban dimension of the Cohesion Policy. One of the reasons is that the Spanish cities that had developed programmes under the first round of URBAN did not have the opportunity to access URBAN II on the basis of a decision taken by the Ministry of Finance (De Gregorio Hurtado, 2012). Nevertheless, the Municipality continued being active in applying for EU funds aiming especially at continuing the regeneration of the historical city centre. During that period it was successful in allocating funds from the Local Operative Programme and INTERREG for that purpose. The funding was almost totally (97%) devoted to urban planning actions, characterized by a physical approach. The total amount devoted to this was 35,433,678 Euros (Barreiro 2013, 21).

The IU was the programme co-funded by the ERDF that, in Spain, made possible the continuation of the experience of URBAN and URBAN II during the 2007–2013 programming period (De Gregorio Hurtado 2018). It corresponds with the period of the Cohesion Policy characterized by the intention of the EC to mainstream the principles of the URBAN Community Initiative in the Operational Programmes of the member states and the regions (European Commission 2008), so that European cities could benefit from the lessons derived from it and apply them to develop an integrated approach to the regeneration of urban areas (Atkinson, 2014). One of the possibilities that the member states had in the 2007–2013 framework to implement this vision was the voluntary use of Article 8 of the ERDF Regulation (EC 1080/2006) entitled 'Sustainable Urban Development'. The application of this article would begin an initiative similar to URBAN but defined and launched by each of the member states. Spain was the only country that decided to create such a specific instrument to operate in cities of all the regions. This policy decision underlines the Spanish case as an interesting exception in the EU framework of that time (De Gregorio Hurtado 2018). It was important because it gave cities the opportunity to continue developing the experience started with URBAN in a country without an explicit national urban policy.

The IU was launched by two calls prepared by the *Dirección General de Fondos Comunitarios* of the Ministry of Finance, restricted to cities with a population of over 50,000 inhabitants and the provincial capitals. The Ministry completely aligned this instrument with Article 8 of the ERDF Regulation, yielding strategies of urban regeneration able to adopt *'an integrated approach for the development of a multidisciplinary set of actions (environmental, social, urban, economic, touristic, cultural, heritage, new technologies, information society, etc.) to address the problems of an urban area selected within the Municipality and at a clear social and economic disadvantage compared to the rest of the city'* (Ministerio de Hacienda, 2007: 1).

Málaga was one of the 46 programmes selected to access the IU. At the beginning of the 2007–2013 period, the Municipality considered that the efforts undertaken through URBAN and the other complementary initiatives in the city centre had contributed visibly to its environmental improvement (Ayuntamiento de Málaga, undated: 2). Nevertheless, the work carried out until that moment had not benefitted the northern part of that area, particularly the neigbourhoods of Ollerías and Lagunillas. Because of this, the decision was made to focus the programme on them (see Figure 4), preparing a proposal based on the experience that the city had developed in the framework of URBAN. In addition, the

Figure 4. Area of development of the IU of Málaga. Source: self-developed based on (Ayuntamiento de Málaga, undated: 3).

experience gained by the Municipality through the development of the Local Agenda 21 and the Strategic Plan was relevant in the preparation of the IU programme.

5.2.1. *Addressing the integrated approach: measures integrated into the Iniciativa Urbana programme and their level of coherence*

The IU call of the Ministerio de Hacienda (2007) suggested to cities that they act in a number of thematic areas (just as in URBAN, it was not compulsory to act in all of them). The strategy proposed by Málaga focused on six on them through the proposal and development of specific measures (Ayuntamiento de Málaga, undated: 37–38) (Table 2):

During this period Málaga also developed the EU action POCTEFEX that complemented the IU programme. Both initiatives, URBAN and POCTEFEX acted mainly through urban actions, including in this case, social and labour-oriented actions, and measures to foster the commercial activity in the area. The total budget devoted (in both of these instruments) to the regeneration of the area amounted to 20,364,789 Euros (Barreiro 2013, 21).

The observation of the measures developed within the IU reveals that, in fact, the city focused again mainly on the physical improvement of the city centre. It is worth mentioning that, along with this 'traditional' approach to urban regeneration, the programme integrated an interest in dealing with 'new' challenges that were being introduced with some difficulty in the policy agenda of local governments in Spain. In

Table 2. Axes of action and measures implemented by the Iniciativa Urbana programme of Málaga. Source: self-developed, based on (Ayuntamiento de Málaga, n.d.).

1. Urban environment
  a. Refurbishment of urban spaces:
    i. Intervention in the area Pozos Dulces-Nosquera.
    ii. Intervention in the area Dos Aceras-Plaza Montaño.
    iii. Intervention in the area Beatas y Tomás de Cózar.
  b. Center for the coordination on action against Climate Change.
  c. Environmental advisory center.
  d. Thematic network for the control of acoustic limiters.
  e. Awareness campaign on cleaning and recycling.
2. Development of the Economic fabric.
  a. Support to existing commercial activity and creation of new initiatives.
  b. Office for the support to entrepreneurs.
3. Infrastructures for services.
  a. Playroom and participation center.
    i. Municipal playroom.
    ii. Area for participative resources.
    iii. Classrooms for equality and citizen education.
  b. Civic Center for community dynamization and organization.
4. Fostering social integration and equal opportunities.
  a. Time Bank.
  b. Training classroom: 'Malaga Participates'.
5. Professional Training.
  a. Project for unemployed labour insertion.
  b. School of women in 'masculinized' professional areas.
6. Management.

this regard, one measure was particularly significant, the creation of a Centre for the Coordination of Climate Change Action. This institution introduced and made visible a relevant policy domain at that moment, showing that Málaga was capable of embedding this topic in urban regeneration, something that few cities in the IU were able to do. The revision of this measure allows us to observe that Málaga took on physical and environmental degeneration whilst keeping an eye on emerging challenges. The Centre was aimed at starting up a dialogue with the economic, social and cultural stakeholders in order to involve them in the local Climate Change strategy. Nowadays, this organization continues to function, but in a limited way. For example, the city is developing its Climate Plan (addressing mitigation, and especially, adaptation to Climate Change), but it is being developed by the OMAU, the Observatory of the Urban Environment of Malaga (interview 1) not by the Centre for the Coordination of Climate Change Action, which shows a limitation in the delivery of local capacity of this concrete measure.

Another innovative approach adopted in Málaga's IU programme was the gender-oriented approach that was introduced by several interrelated actions, something that many cities participating in the IU were not able to carry out in a consistent way (ibid.).

With regard to the general adoption of an integrated approach, the document of proposal with which the Municipality accessed the IU stated that *'it was not conceivable to carry out actions of physical rehabilitation of streets, squares or buildings, without developing at the same time actions of social integration, professional training or promotion of economic development and employment'* (Ayuntamiento de Málaga, undated: 32). It also remarked that the strategy of urban regeneration proposed was innovative because of the adoption of this integrated vision. Nevertheless, as mentioned, the programme adopted a vision that significantly prioritised the physical renovation of buildings and the public space under a traditional approach. The integrated vision was present in the discourse but not fully embedded in the specific measures. The integrated approach embedded in the IU of Málaga was again characterized by a lack of coherence.

In this framework, the result of the set of actions undertaken by the programme proved that the goal of physical regeneration of the area was reached. However, the social and economic improvements were not (interview 1). This limitation is notably visible in the decrease in the population in the area as a result of the 'touristification' trend that it is undergoing (Marín, Guevara, and Navarro-Jurado 2017). A study carried out by the OMAU (2013) shows that the physical improvement of the city centre has resulted in it being established as a location for leisure activities, such as pubs and restaurants, and services for tourists. The concentration of these activities is creating noise, waste, and a lack of local commerce and services for the inhabitants, which encourages the residents that can afford to, to abandon the area. The study also indicates that people living in Málaga and visiting the city centre actively appreciated it in terms of leisure and beauty, but would not consider it as a residential option (ibíd.). This issue is relevant in the framework of this study and establishes that the urban regeneration programmes need to address the recovery of the areas whilst including measures to prevent 'touristification' and/or massive gentrification (particularly in the city centers). The example of Málaga introduces this important topic for reflection and action in the framework of the urban policy of the EU.

5.2.2. The governance model put into place to define and implement the regeneration strategy

The programme included in its strategy the participation of the local stakeholders as a crucial element. This shows significant progress when compared to the approach embedded in the URBAN programme some years before. The proposal prepared by the Municipality to access the IU stated that 'its success depended largely on the ability to broker agreements between different stakeholders in the definition of objectives and priorities' (Ayuntamiento de Málaga, undated: 31). For that, the programme aimed to reinforce the participative mechanisms that were being developed in the area during that period. This is something that was done by many of the programmes of the IU developed in Spain (Author 2018).

In the city centre of Málaga, the participatory mechanisms focused on the Consejo Territorial de Participación del Distrito Centro (Territorial Council for Participation in the City Centre) that was integrated by 23 associations and entities (Ayuntamiento de Málaga, undated: 31). For the participation of these actors, the programme established the creation of the 'Assembly Iniciativa Urbana Arrabales'. The process of urban participation foresaw the development of coordination and monitoring meetings (the first meeting of the Assembly took place in March 2008), setting a minimum of two meetings per year. This was complemented by an online platform aimed at providing information on the programme, so that the different actors could study it before the meetings (interview 1). The methodology of participation also included the development of interviews aimed at identifying the degree of satisfaction in the measures undertaken by the programme (ibid.).

In order to develop local capacity based on the knowledge and involvement of the local stakeholders in the programme, the strategy planned the direct management of some actions by social entities working in the area.

The participation of the local community was also integrated into the programme's strategy as a specific axis (axis 5: Female culture and citizens participation). It included an action of training in citizen participation called 'Málaga Participa' located in a new facility to be constructed in the framework of the programme. The goal of this measure was to mainstream citizen's participation, the gender perspective, the sustainable urban development approach and multicultural diversity in the urban regeneration strategy (Ayuntamiento de Málaga, undated).

The URBAN programme (1994–1999) and the participative work developed in the framework of the Strategic Plan and the Local Agenda 21 of the city resulted in the construction of local capacity (particularly institutional capacity) to produce a solid public participation process in the context of the IU. Proof of this is that the strategy developed for public participation aimed at integrating the view of the local actors, but also at actively involving them in the management of some crucial measures.

5.3. *The EDUSI of Malaga (2014–2020)*

For the 2014–2020 period of the Cohesion Policy, the urban axis was reinforced. In trying to overcome some of the problems identified in the previous experience and direct the initiative to a more results-based programme, relevant novelties were introduced (De Luca 2016). Another important difference was the introduction of the obligation of the member states to ring-fence a minimum 5% of the ERDF for integrated sustainable urban development. This was established by the Article 7 of the ERDF regulation that allowed the countries to make different arrangements for this within their Operational Programmes. Spain decided to develop a specific priority axis dedicated to sustainable urban development for which the experience acquired previously, through the URBAN and the URBAN II Community Initiatives and the IU, was crucial (interviews 2 and 3).

Even if the EDUSI call was defined by the Ministry with the support of a task group that developed this activity building on the knowledge amassed through the implementation of the previous instruments (interview 3), it is worth noting that the EDUSI presented important differences when compared with URBAN and the IU. This was because of the approach adopted by the EU with regard to the urban dimension of Cohesion Policy for 2014–2020, which was embedded in documents such as the one entitled *Guidance for Member States on Integrated Sustainable Urban Development* (European Commission 2016), that established neat differences in regard to previous instruments. When compared to them, the new vision appears more focused on fostering urban competitiveness than on supporting cities in facing urban deprivation in their more vulnerable neighbourhoods, something that contrasts with the difficulties that cities were facing in 2014, in the context of the economic crisis, when the programming period started. The most relevant differences are the following:

- The EDUSI call did not establish an obligation to act in the most vulnerable areas of cities.
- The EDUSI call did not propose an area-based approach. It was voluntary to adopt it as cities could distribute the actions to be undertaken in different parts of their territory.

- Cities had to propose action within the Thematic Objectives set by the Cohesion Policy for the 2014–2020 period. In the framework of the agreement between Spain and the European Commission (Ministerio de Economía y Administraciones Públicas, undated), Spain decided to focus urban instruments on the Thematic Objectives 2, 4, 6, and 9 in order to achieve the goals set in the *Europe 2020 Strategy* (interview 2).

For the development of the EDUSI, Málaga proposed to act again in the historic centre (see Figure 5): The document developed to access the call justified this because the area still presented socio-economic and physical indicators below the city's average (that were being monitored in the framework of the Agenda 21), and because it had been identified as a vulnerable area by different entities (Ministry of Public Works, Complutense University, and Andalusian Region) (OMAU, 2015, 17). This highlights the fact that, even if addressing vulnerability was not a priority set by the call, Málaga decided to adopt an approach in line with the experience gained through URBAN and the IU, focusing on a vulnerable neighbourhood. At that stage, the city centre had been identified as an area of opportunity, in which the regeneration programme could attract further investment.

Regarding the area selected, the approach adopted by the EDUSI of Málaga is not based on an area-based vision, demonstrating in this case an important difference between it and the

Figure 5. Area of development of the EDUSI of Málaga. Source: self-developed based on (Ayuntamiento de Málaga, 2016).

IU and URBAN programmes. The comparison of Figures 2, 3, and 4 presents a greater level of homogeneity in the first initiatives as well as an intention to concentrate the financial and technical efforts in smaller areas in which the 'leverage effect' could be an important factor.

5.3.1. *Addressing the integrated approach: measures integrated into the EDUSI and their level of coherence*

As mentioned, the EDUSI call was contextualized in the framework of the urban dimension of the Cohesion Policy 2014–2020 in which cities had to concentrate their action on four Thematic Objectives (Ayuntamiento de Málaga 2016) (Table 3).

Based on the measures included, the EDUSI of Málaga reveals a notable level of similarity regarding the integrated approach to the URBAN and IU programmes. It has been able to produce a set of urban regeneration measures that focus on the physical dimension, as well as integrating smart city and carbon reduction approaches. It is

Table 3. Thematic Objectives and actions implemented by the EDUSI of Málaga. Source: self-developed, based on (Ayuntamiento de Málaga, 2016).

Thematic Objective 2 (TO2): Improvement of the use and quality of ICT:
  a. Promotion of ICT in the strategies of integrated sustainable development through the local electronic administration and open government.
  b. Smart Cities:
    i. Water meter reading.
    ii. Use of Near Field Communication (NFC) in touristic and cultural attractions.
    iii. Management of bus circulation (SAE system).
    iv. Mobility information panels.
    v. Control of heavy vehicles by laser and cameras.
    vi. Incident information system in public transport.

Thematic Objective 4 (TO4): Favour alow carbon economy:
  a. Improvement of public transport and sustainable mobility:
  b. Provision of small modal interchanges.
    i. New line of high capacity bus.
  c. Improvement of the road and pedestrian connections.
    i. Greenway cyclist and pedestrian pathway Guadalmedina.
    ii. Action in the area Carretería-Álamos.
  d. Improvement of energy efficiency and increase of renewable energy.
    i. Improvement of energy efficiency in public housing.
    ii. LED lighting in parking and bus stops.

Thematic Objective 6 (TO6): Urban environment and cultural heritage:
  a. Value of the historical and tourist heritage.
    i. Remodeling of tourism information points.
    ii. Illuminated route of mural paintings in Malaga.
  b. Improvement of cultural structures.
    i. Signs and digitization Alcazaba-Gibralfaro.
    ii. Glass Museum and archeological interpretation center.
  c. Improvement of the urban environment.
    i. Recovery of the environment and public space Lagunillas, SOHO, Trinidad-Perchel and El Ejido.
    ii. Plan of quiet acoustic zones.

Thematic Objective 9 (TO9): Promotion of social inclusion and fight against urban poverty:
  a. Physical, economic and social regeneration of vulnerable areas:
    i. Action in Plaza de los Filipenses.
    ii. Senior Center in Plaza de Paula.
  b. Social welfare and citizen participation.
    i. School of citizenship.
    ii. Comprehensive care and employment service.
  c. Promotion of business activity and self-employment.
    i. Entrepreneurship Center Llano de la Trinidad.
    ii. Renovation of the Salamanca Market.
    iii. Soho Investor Programme.

remarkable that the programme does this with a relevant level of concretion when compared with other municipalities that are also currently implementing EDUSI programmes. In fact, one of the most relevant limitations of the EDUSI model is that it focuses on general strategies that cities need to further develop in a second policy stage. At the end of 2018, this resulted in the cities having difficulties to comply with the agreed upon level of economic expense (interview 2). The definition of the EDUSI of Málaga reveals the capacity developed through previous urban regeneration experiences, presenting: i) a high level of concretion of the measures to be developed; ii) a valuable capacity to integrate new topics (particularly concentrated in the TO2 and TO4) in urban development strategies.

Even if the programme successfully integrates measures in different dimensions, the compulsory thematic-concentration adopted by the EDUSI call has limited the integrated approach in the proposal, as the instrument cannot fund measures in all the relevant axes of urban decline. This obstacle to develop holistic strategies should be avoided in the design of the post-2020 urban instruments co-financed by the Cohesion Policy of the EU.

5.3.2. *The governance model put into place to define and implement the regeneration strategy*

The EDUSI call, launched by the Ministry, required the adoption of a participative approach for the elaboration, implementation and monitoring of the strategies (RIU, 2015). Málaga complied with this by applying the lessons learnt from previous urban instruments co-financed by the Cohesion Policy and other instruments. In fact, at the moment of the preparation of the proposal, the Municipality pointed out that the EDUSI was being constructed on the basis of key instruments such as the Urban Agenda and the Strategic Plan (Ayuntamiento 2016). In any case, the development of the EDUSI strategy involved the preparation of a specific participation strategy (Observatorio de Medio Ambiente Urbano, OMAU 2015, 141–148) based on three dimensions:

- Transversal participation in local management (collaboration between the different government areas of the Municipality).
- Participation of the Municipality and the social and economic stakeholders.
- Participation of the Municipality and the citizens.

These mechanisms allowed to integrate the requirements of the different agents in the strategy, introducing changes in the draft previously prepared by the Municipality. To be concrete, they allowed contact with 493 associations and other social agents. Some of them participated in the different activities mentioned and in other participative meetings (ibid: 142–143). The participation strategy has also produced mechanisms aimed at maintaining the presence of the stakeholders and the citizens during the implementation and monitoring[2] of the EDUSI. This strategy is being developed at the moment, so it's impossible to predict its results. What can be asserted, thanks to the analysis developed for this article, is that the participative strategy has evolved significantly when compared with previous instruments, showing that it is well rooted in the programme and integrated with the different actions. This demonstrates that the experience acquired by the municipality has delivered local capacity in this regard.

Conclusions

The study shows an evolution over time in the development of the specific instruments funded under the umbrella of the urban dimension of Cohesion Policy in Málaga that can be considered as having contributed to the development of local capacity in the city, particularly to technical and institutional capacity. This has been confirmed by the stakeholder of the Municipality of Málaga that was interviewed (interview 1) and the literature reviewed, as well as through the comparison of the instruments analysed. In fact, it is possible to observe a growing internal coherence regarding the analytical categories studied in the different instruments. In this regard, it is relevant to point out that the documents prepared by Málaga to access all the instruments analysed (URBAN, IU, and EDUSI) had been developed by the Municipality. This is something that sets it apart from other cities, especially those participating in the EDUSI call, as most of the strategies had been developed by consultants. This proves that over time the city has developed in-house knowledge that allows it to develop strategies able to compete for EU funding.

The analysis undertaken also reveals that the implementation of other instruments, particularly the Local Agenda 21 and the Strategic Plan, has contributed in a synergic way to enhance the approach and the results of the EU instruments analysed. The city has also been very active in developing other instruments and policies, for example in the field of sustainable urban mobility and smart solutions. These have been implemented in parallel to the EU instruments analysed. The lessons learnt through these initiatives have resulted in mutual benefits and a more holistic vision. The sustained monitoring of the city's urban reality (in the context of its urban agenda and its strategic plan) has been an important factor for this, as it has provided the information necessary to make an integrated diagnosis able to support holistic urban regeneration strategies for the city centre.

The urban instruments funded through the Cohesion Policy have contributed to the development of local capacity in the implementation of an integrated urban regeneration method . This knowledge has become embedded in the practices of the Municipality thanks to experience accumulated over 25 years, and has contributed to avoid some of the limitations of the EDUSI scheme.

The discourse adopted by the documents developed in the framework of the instruments that have been analysed reveals that in Málaga there was an early understanding of the model of urban regeneration that was proposed by the European Commission at the beginning of the 1990s, and that there has been a positive evolution in the way in which this model has been embedded in the technical urban and policy discourse of the Municipality. The continuation of this approach over time also helps to identify a political will and commitment to make this issue visible, contributing to the perception of Málaga as one of the most active and innovative Spanish cities in addressing sustainable urban development. The adoption of this model goes beyond the discourse, being present also in the urban sustainability policy developed by the city from the 1990s onwards. Nevertheless, in this regard, the analysis identifies highly visible inertias, limitations, and contradictions in the implementation of the instruments studied and their results in the city centre. These inconsistencies are also visible in the policy action undertaken throughout the 25 years analysed, in which Málaga has positioned itself as a city committed to sustainable urban development, and at the same has continued to foster urban expansion, the consumption of land, the real state sector's intense activity (particularly before the economic crisis of 2007–2008) and the enhancement of the tourist sector, prioritizing it over environmental sustainability (Marín 2000).

The different instruments analysed demonstrate relevant progress in the way in which the participation of the local community has been integrated, ranging from an informative approach in the URBAN programme (1994–1999) to an articulated and institutionalized process of public participation able to create local capacity in the EDUSI (2014–2020). Regarding the integrated approach, the priority given to the physical dimension has determined the partial results achieved by all the instruments: the city centre still presents relevant social problems, even if the urban environment has greatly improved. In this regard, the case of Málaga sheds light on some of the limitations and inconsistencies of the urban development model that is being fostered by the EU. It provides lessons that could lead to a reflection in the framework of the negotiations for the definition of the urban axis of the Cohesion Policy for the 2021–27 period. The lack of a strong social dimension in the urban instruments, in which economic competitiveness has over time become more intense, and the attention paid to the improvement of the quality of the urban space have attracted leisure and commercial activities for tourists to the city centre. This, along with the persistence of social problems, is resulting in the abandonment of the area by its original population. Beyond this, in the case of the EDUSI programmes, the thematic concentration required by the Cohesion Policy rules has added a new level of difficulty in addressing in an integrated way the most relevant problems of the area.

The study carried out shows that the EU instruments supported by the urban dimension of the Cohesion Policy can greatly impact the urban policy approach of cities, bringing about awareness and local capacity with regard to relevant issues related to the sustainable regeneration of existing vulnerable neighbourhoods. The case of Málaga demonstrates the benefits of this vision. Nevertheless, at the same time, exogenous factors related to the need for cities to attract financial investment can significantly hinder the effects of the transformative capacity undertaken through Cohesion Policy instruments. They limit the delivery potential of the knowledge and experience amassed by local institutions and actors and can result in undesired effects.

The lessons that emerge from the analysis of the case of Málaga make some recommendations to be taken into account in the medium term, and particularly in the design of urban instruments under the urban dimension of Cohesion Policy for the post-2020 period. It is important to 'recover' the area-based approach and to go beyond it, fostering the social dimension of the initiatives undertaken through an people-based approach, and reinforcing the request of coherence among the EU instruments and the local policies. This is particularly important to prevent gentrification and the touristification of the city centres in which Cohesion Policy acts. It is also necessary to reinforce the request of specific conditions to access EU funding (for example, the integration in the regeneration strategies of an explicit and coherent integrated approach, a collaborative governance model, and a sound participatory framework to implement the strategies), and to reinforce the capacity-building dimension (introducing it as an explicit objective). The study undertaken also shows the relevance of overcoming the thematic concentration proposed by Cohesion Policy in the current period. In this regard, it is important to find a balance among the EU's policy priorities and the needed flexibility of the instruments to be able to address urban complexity in very different national contexts. The way in which the definition of the urban dimension of Cohesion Policy for the 2021–27 period is advancing seems to be a continuation of the approach adopted for the 2014–20 period. This study aims to contribute to a reflection on these issues in the present and crucial decision-making context for the cities of the EU.

Notes

1. For example, Portugal developed the programmes Polis (2000) and Polis XXI (2007) (Cavaco et al. 2019), Italy developed programmes such as the Contratti di Quartiere (1998) (Governa & Salone 2005; Vinci 2019).
2. The main mechanisms are the following:

    - Annual assembly for the monitoring of the EDUSI, counting on the presence of the associations of the area and the citizens. It will evaluate the strategy on the basis of participative tools and yield proposals.
    - Use of the online platform, social networks and media to announce the results.
    - Use of the participative web EDUSI 2015 during the EDUSI's active life to regularly gather proposals developed by different agents.
    - Sectoral meetings with specific task groups.
    - Sectoral table for the participation of citizens in the area of action. It will work as the secretary for the participative process.

Acknowledgements

The author thanks the stakeholders that provided information: Interview 1: Pedro Marín (Director of the Observatorio de Medio Ambiente Urbano de Málaga) on the 23-10-2018; Interview 2: Lola Ortiz (Subdirectora General de Desarrollo Urbano of the Ministerio de Hacienda y Función Pública), and Interview 3: Emilia Martínez Urritia (Jefa de Servicio in the Ministerio de Hacienda y Función Pública) on the 27-6-2018.

Disclosure statement

No potential conflict of interest was reported by the author.

References

Adshead, M. 2014. "EU Cohesion Policy and Multi-level Governance Outcomes in Ireland: How Sustainable Is Europeanization?" *European Urban and Regional Studies* 21 (4): 416–431. doi:10.1177/0969776413490426.

Armondi, S., and S. De Gregorio Hurtado. 2019. *Foregrounding Urban Agendas: The New Urban Issue in European Experiences of Policy-making*. Cham: Springer.

Atkinson, R., and A. Walliser. 2013. "Do We Really Want to Learn? EU Funded Urban Programmes and Their Impact on Urban Regeneration, Knowledge and Learning in Madrid." In *Production and Use of Urban Knowledge*, edited by R. Atkinson and H. T. Andersen, 133–150. London: Springer.

Atkinson, R. 2014. "*The Urban Dimension in Cohesion Policy: Past Developments and Future Prospects.*" Paper presented at RSA workshop on 'The New Cycle of the Cohesion Policy in 2014–2020', Institute for European Studies, Vrije Universitetit Brussels, 24 March 2014.

Ayuntamiento de Malaga 2015. *Estrategia Urbana Integrada Sostenible "Perchel Lagunillas"*. Málaga: Ayuntamiento de Málaga. Accessed 23 August 2018. http://edusi.malaga.eu/opencms/export/sites/feder/.content/galerias/documentos/eDUSI-Perchel-Lagunillas.pdf

Ayuntamiento de Malaga. 2016. *Viva La Calle. URBAN 1994–2016, 22 Años De Recuperación Del Centro Histórico. La Nueva EDUSI 2017–2022*. Málaga: Ayuntamiento de Málaga.

Ayuntamiento de Malaga. n.d. *Arrabales Y Carreterías. Iniciativa Urbana Málaga 2007–2013*. Málaga: Ayuntamiento de Málaga.

Barreiro, F. 2013. *Evaluación De Los Impactos Del Proceso De Recuperación Y Regeneración Urbana Integral Del Centro Histórico De Málaga*. Málaga: OMAU.

Borja, J. 2002. "Participación, Un Desafío, Una Oportunidad, Una Cuestión Política." In *Diagnóstico. Proyecto Educativo De Ciudad*, edited by Ayuntamiento de Gijón, 95–106. Gijón: Ayuntamiento de Gijón.

Campos Venuti, G. 1987. *La Terza Generazione Dell'urbanistica*. Milan: Franco Angeli.

Carpenter, J. 2006. "Addressing Europe's urban challenges: Lessons from the EU Urban Community Initiative." *Urban Studies* 43 (12): 2145–2162.

Carpenter, J. 2013. "Sustainable Urban Regeneration within the European Union. A Case of 'europeanization'?" In *The Routledge Companion to Urban Regeneration*, edited by E. M. Leary and J. McCarthy, 138–147. London: Routledge.

Cavaco, C., R. Florentino, and A. Pagliuso. 2019. "Urban Policies in Portugal." In *Foregrounding Urban Agendas: The New Urban Issue in European Experiences of Policy-making*, edited by S. Armondiand De Gregorio Hurtado. Cham: Springer.

Cotella, G., and U. Janin Rivolin. 2011. "Europeanization of Spatial Planning through Discourse and Practice in Italy." *disP – The Planning Review* 47 (3): 42–53. doi:10.1080/02513625.2011.10557143.

De Gregorio Hurtado, S. 2012. "URBAN Policies of the European Union from the Perspective of Collaborative Planning. The URBAN and URBAN II Community Initiatives in Spain." PhD Thesis., Universidad Politécnica de Madrid. doi:10.1094/PDIS-11-11-0999-PDN.

De Gregorio Hurtado, S. 2014. "La Iniciativa Comunitaria URBAN Como Factor De transformación de la práctica de la regeneración urbana. aproximación al caso español." *Ciudad Y Territorio. Estudios Territoriales* 180: 153–175.

De Gregorio Hurtado, S. 2017a. "Is EU Urban Policy Transforming Urban Regeneration in Spain? Answers from an Analysis of the Iniciativa Urbana (2007–2013)." *Cities* 60: 402–414. doi:10.1016/j.cities.2016.10.015.

De Gregorio Hurtado, S. 2017b. ""La Política Urbana De La Unión Europea En España." *De URBAN a Las EDUSI", TRIA –territorio Della Ricerca Su Insediamenti E Ambiente-* 18: 47–74.

De Gregorio Hurtado, S. 2018. "The EU Urban Policy in the Period 2007–2013: Lessons from the Spanish Experience." *Regional Studies, Regional Science* 5 (1): 212–230. doi:10.1080/21681376.2018.1480903.

De Luca, S. 2016. "Politiche Europee E Città: Stato Dell'arte E Prospettive Future", *Working papers. Rivista online di Urban@it*, 2/2016. Accessed 1 October 2018. http://www.urbanit.it/wp-content/uploads/2016/10/6_BP_De_Luca_S.pdf

Del Castillo, J., and S. N. Haarich.2013. "Informe Final." Estudio sobre el "Desarrollo Urbano Sostenible co-financiado por el FEDER en España 2014–2020: Directirces Estratégicas y Prioridades de Inversión. Las Arenas: Infyde.

Dukes, T. 2008. "The URBAN Programme and the European URBAN Policy Discourse: Successful Instruments to Europeanize the URBAN Level?" *GeoJournal* 72 (1–2): 105–119. doi:10.1007/s10708-008-9168-2.

Ertan, T., and Y. Eercioglu. 2016. "Historic City Center Urban Regeneration: The Case of Malaga and Kemeralti, Izmir." *Procedia Social and Behavioral Sciences* 223 (2016): 601–607. doi:10.1016/j.sbspro.2016.05.362.

European Commission. 1994: "*Notice to the Member States Laying down Guidelines for Operational Programmes Which Member States are Invited to Establish in the Framework of a Community Initiative Concerning Urban Areas (URBAN)*." DOCE nº L 180/37, 01 July 1994, pp. 06–09. Commission of the European Communities.

European Commission. 2008. *Fostering the Urban Dimension. Analysis of the Operational Programmes Co-financed by the European Regional Development Fund (2007-2013)*. Brussels: Working Document of the Directorate-General for Regional Policy. Commission of the European Communities.

European Commission. 2016. *Guidance for Member States on Integrated Sustainable Urban Development (Article 7 ERDF regulation)*. Brussels: Commission of the European Communities.

European Commission. 2009. *Promoting Sustainable Development in Europe. Achievements and Opportunities*. Brussels: Commission of the European Communities.

Ferrary, M. 2010: "Uno De Cada Cuatro Edificios De Málaga Se Ha Construido En Los Últimos Diez Años". La Opinión de Málaga. 15 September 2010.

González Medina, M., S. De Gregorio Hurtado, J. Carpenter, and M. A. Huete. 2017. "Europeización y Política Urbana de la UE: Impacto en las Agendas nacionales de España, Francia, Italia, y Renio Unido". In *La fortaleza de Europea. Vallas y puentes* edited by XIII Congreso AECPA. Santiago de Compostela, 20-22th September 2017.

Governa, F., and C. Salone. 2005. "Italy and European Spatial Policies: Polycentrism, Urban Networks and Local Innovation Practices." *European Planning Studies* 13 (2): 265–283.

Hall, P. 1987. "Las Ciudades De Europa." ¿Un Problema Europeo? ¿Una Profesión Europea? *Urbanismo* 1: 25–31.

Healey, P. 1997. *Collaborative Planning*. New York: Palgrave Macmillan.

Marín, P. 2000. "Programas Para La Mejora Del Medioambiente Urbano En La Ciudad De Málaga." *Informes De La Construcción* 51 (465): 25–34. doi:10.3989/ic.2000.v51.i465.

Marín, P., A. Guevara, and E. Navarro-Jurado. 2017. "Renovación Urbana Y Masificación Turística En La Ciudad Antigua: Pérdida De Población Y Conflictos Sociales." *En Ciudad Y Territorio. Estudios Territoriales* 193: 453–468.

Ministerio de Hacienda. 2007. *Iniciativa Urbana (URBAN). Orientaciones Para La Elaboración De Propuestas*. Madrid: Ministerio de Economía y Hacienda

Ministerio de Hacienda. 2003a. *Informe Final Del Programa Operativo URBAN 1994-1999*. Madrid: Ministerio de Hacienda.

Ministerio de Hacienda. 2003b. *Informe Final Del Programa Operativo URBAN 1997-1999*. Madrid: Ministerio de Hacienda.

Observatorio de Medio Ambiente Urbano, OMAU. 2013. *Campaña De Encuestas Para La Evaluación Externa De Las Actuaciones Y Del Proceso De Renovación Integral Del PEPRI Centro*. Málaga: Estudio 7 SL.

Observatorio de Medio Ambiente Urbano, OMAU. 2015. *Estrategia Urbana Integrada Sostenible "Perchel Lagunillas"*. Málaga: OMAU.

Parkinson, M., S. De Gregorio Hurtado, and C. Lefèvre. 2013. "National Policy Spain." In *Second Tier Cities and Territorial Development in Europe: Performance, Policies and Prospects*, edited by M. Parkinson, 179–206, ESPON. Retrieved from: https://www.espon.eu/sites/default/files/attachments/SGPTD_Final_Report_-_Final_Version_27.09.12.pdf

Prointec. 2000. *Estudio De Evaluación Intermedia Del Programa Operativo URBAN I. Volumen I: Análisis De Los Proyectos Individuales De Cada Ciudad*. Madrid: Ministerio de Economía y Hacienda.

Red de Iniciativas Urbanas, RIU. 2015. *Orientaciones Para La Definición De Estrategias De Desarrollo Urbano Sostenible Integrado En El Periodo 2014-2020*. Madrid: Red de Iniciativas Urbanas.

Roberts, P., and H. Sykes. (2000). Urban Regeneration. *A handbook*. London: Sage Publications.

Romero, J. 2005. "El Gobierno Del Territorio En España. Balance De Iniciativas De Coordinación Y Cooperación Territorial." *Boletín De La AGE* 39: 59–86.

Sainz Gutiérrez, V. 2006. *El Proyecto Urbano En España: Génesis Y Desarrollo De Un Urbanismo De Los Arquitectos*. Sevilla: Universidad de Sevilla.

Tofarides, M. 2003. *Urban Policy in the European Union: A Multi-Level Gatekeeper System*. Aldershot; Burlington: Ashgate.

Tortola, P. D. 2016. "Europeanization in Time: Assessing the Legacy of URBAN in a Mid-size Italian City." *European Planning Studies* 24 (1): 96–115. doi:10.1080/09654313.2015.1062083.

Urrutia, V. 1992. "Transformación Y Persistencia De Los Movimientos Sociales Urbanos." *Política Y Sociedad* 4: 49–56.

Vinci, I. 2019. "Governing the metropolitan dimension. A critical perspective on institutional reshaping and planning innovation in Italy." *European Journal of Spatial Development* 70. Retrieved from: https://www.nordregio.org/publications/governing-the-metropolitan-dimension-a-critical-perspective-on-institutional-reshaping-and-planning-innovation-in-italy/

How the EU regional policy can shape urban change in Southern Europe: learning from different planning processes in Palermo

Ignazio Vinci

ABSTRACT
The article provides an interpretation of the role played by the EU regional policy in the process of urban change experienced in Palermo, the fifth Italian city by population and capital of one of the largest Europe's less developed regions (Sicily). Through an analysis of various EU-funded planning initiatives implemented over the last two decades – from the Urban Community Initiative in the late nineties to the current Integrated Territorial Investments under the 2014–2020 urban agenda –, the work explores their effects from three main perspectives: urban regeneration, local governance, and planning innovation.

1. Introduction

The links between regional and urban development started to be explicitly addressed in the European Community after the reform of the Structural Funds approved in 1988. In fact, such reform has meant not only a deep reconfiguration of the rationale and functioning of what now we call Cohesion Policy (Bachtler et al. 2017; Piattoni and Polverari 2016), but also a clearer recognition of cities as drivers for European regional development (EC 2011a, 2014a; McCann 2015). As a result, while the EU has never assumed urban policy among its formal competencies, from the nineties onward cities were the target of growing interest, both from a political and operational standpoint.

The emergence of an urban dimension in the EU regional policy, now widely addressed in literature (Atkinson 2015; Atkinson and Zimmermann 2016; Carpenter 2013; Dossi 2017; Hamedinger and Wolffhardt 2010; Parkinson 2006; Medeiros 2019) and in a range of official policy documents (EC 1997, 1998, 2008, 2009, 2011b, 2014b; EP 2005, 2014), can be described as the result of the interactions of two main processes: (a) on the one hand, the creation of programmes and financial instruments specifically targeted on cities, such as the Urban Pilot Projects (1990–1999), the Urban Community Initiative (1994–2006) or Jessica (2007–2013); (b) on the other, the increasing attention granted to urban development within the ordinary instruments of Cohesion Policy, notably Structural Funds.

Despite the fact that both channels still represent the main ways sustainable urban development is promoted by the European Union, in the last decade, the direct support to the city's planning initiatives (i.e. Urban) has been gradually replaced by programmes and networks mostly aimed at the dissemination of data (Urban Audit) or best practices across the European cities (Urbact). On the contrary, from the period 2007–2013, a growing number of national and regional operational programmes in the framework of Cohesion Policy are characterized by the presence of thematic objectives related to urban development (EC 2008). The effects of this process, so far documented only by a few systematic analyses (ECORYS 2010; Ramsden and Colini 2013), seems to be expanding in the 2014–2020 programming cycle (van der Zwet et al. 2017). For instance, Matko (2016) found that in this period, at least 114 operational programmes present an explicit reference to urban issues and several member states have agreed to address the Integrated Territorial Investments (under article 36 of the ERDF's Regulation) over the main urban areas. Overall, Medeiros and van der Zwet (2019) estimate that in 2014–2020, around 40% of the European Regional Development Fund (ERDF) will be spent within cities, clearly much beyond the 5% that was required for integrated sustainable urban development by the ERDF's regulation.

To understand the role played by Cohesion Policy, however, such a wide sources for urban development has a series of relevant analytical implications. Firstly, as cities are the target of different types of intervention – area-based integrated action plans, large infrastructure projects, other projects aimed at the provision of services of urban relevance (i.e. green areas, public facilities, etc.) –, urban change should be interpreted as the result of different approaches and planning priorities, often not explicitly coordinated and with diverse spatial articulations. Secondly, since in any given city the EU planning initiatives are part of a wider policy-making process, the analyses in the long term must consider the impact of any changes in local politics, which in turn may lead to changes in development strategies and also in the governance relations.

With these questions as the backdrop, this article seeks to understand which role the EU urban and regional policies have played in the changing process experienced in the city of Palermo, the fifth Italian city by population and capital of one of the largest Europe's less developed region (Sicily). Southern Italy – the 'Italian Mezzogiorno' – is widely recognized as one of the most controversial cases for regional development in the European Union (Leonardi 2005). In fact, after decades of extensive interventions under Cohesion Policy, in the South of Italy major regions such as Campania and Sicily itself have never changed their status from 'less developed regions'. Urban areas within these regions, therefore, reflect – and to some extent are an expression of – all the development problems the EU regional policy has aimed to address from the beginning: infrastructures gaps, lack of competitiveness, weak economic processes, social exclusion.

Following a qualitative approach, the EU initiatives are discussed in the present case study under two main analytical perspectives: (a) for their efficiency/effectiveness in achieving their planned goals and (b) as drivers of 'indirect' effects on local policy-making and the city's transformation process. The sources used for the investigation are, therefore, different types of data and materials: planning documents and evaluation reports, several interviews with relevant stakeholders and other details taken by the (few) contributions found in the literature.

Without any intention to give a comprehensive response to all of them, the research has tried to address the following main research questions:

(1) Have the EU projects provided any recognizable effects on the trajectories of the city's development? Is there any urban area where physical regeneration or socioeconomic revitalization can be directly or indirectly related to the EU initiatives? Is there any policy-field where this influence is clearer?
(2) Can we identify a clear influence of the EU planning initiatives on local governance? How have local stakeholders been involved in the planning processes? Have public–private partnership been effective?
(3) Have the EU projects brought new planning capacities to the local government? To which extent have the European approaches and methods to sustainable urban development been embedded within local policy-making?

This paper is structured as follows. After this introduction, in the second section, the process through which, from the nineties onward, cities in Italy became an object for national policy in the context of the European integration is critically discussed. The third section is entirely devoted to the case study, following a timeline that reflects the main steps in the city's transformation process: from the nineties, when the first EU-led initiatives were implemented in the context of radical political changes, to the present period, when (after the crisis) part of the urban development priorities were reconsidered. The last section of the paper, by summing the city's development process in the last twenty years, seeks to create a cross-the-board perspective of the observed planning experiences, as well as to draw some conclusions being related to the research questions.

2. The Italian urban policy in the context of the Europeanisation process

Europeanisation is a concept shared by many disciplines, that can take several meanings depending on the cultural context it is placed in. According to Radaelli, it can be described as a «process involving (a) construction, (b) diffusion and (c) institutionalization of formal and informal rules, procedures, policy paradigms, styles, 'ways of doing things' and shared beliefs and norms which are first defined and consolidated in the EU policy process and then incorporated in the logic of domestic (national and subnational) discourse, political structures and public choices» (Radaelli 2003, 30). By other scholars, such as (Olsen 2002), Europeanisation is described also as a multidirectional process where the reshaping of national politics and policy-making under the EU influence is accompanied by a bottom-up and even horizontal transfer of knowledge, paradigms and best practices that are increasingly shared within a multi-level governance system. It is from this latter perspective, particularly, that many works in literature (Carpenter 2013; Dossi 2017; Hamedinger and Wolffhardt 2010) have described the emergence of an EU urban policy as a case of Europeanisation.

The rise of a European dimension in Italian urban policy-making is a process that needs to be adequately placed within the broader process which, during the nineties, strengthened the role of cities within the national political system (Artioli 2016). In turn, it is the consequence of two main driving forces supported by large political consensus:

- The decentralization of powers to cities' government, as a result of legal reforms aimed at broadening the autonomy and competencies of local authorities within the institutional system;
- The proactive role of cities towards a series of programmes launched by national government to stimulate local innovation in urban policy-making according to the approach promoted by the EU.

The granting of new powers to cities is the result of legal interventions following different aims and rationality, including laws (a) to redefine the role and functions of local authorities (Law N. 142/1990), (b) to introduce the direct election of mayors, providing larger autonomy to city councils and broader space to participation in collective choices (Law N. 81/1993) and (c) to reshape the organization of local authorities according to simplified procedures and a more explicit managerialist approach to government (Laws N. 59/1997, N. 127/97 and N. 191/98).

It has been argued that these reforms have implied for many Italian cities not only the emergence of new political leadership and increased stability for local government (Vandelli 2000; Vesperini 2000), but also since they created the preconditions for the setting up of clearer urban agendas (Cremaschi 2003; Pasqui 2005).

Many authors have argued (Avarello and Ricci 2000; Governa and Salone 2005; Janin Rivolin 2003; Ombuen, Ricci, and Segnalini 2000) that such return of cities in the political agenda wouldn't have been possible without the great investment made at national level in a new generation of urban programmes promoted since the early nineties. In fact, in a relatively short time, the Italian government launched several funding schemes to help cities to face two challenges largely unexplored in national/local policy, namely (a) neighborhood regeneration and (b) urban competitiveness.

The first challenge has been addressed by national initiatives such as the Urban Recovery Programmes (Programmi di Recupero Urbano – 1993), the Urban Renewal Programmes (Programmi di Riqualificazione Urbana – 1994) or the Neighborhood Contracts (Contratti di Quartiere – 1997). These programmes mostly focused on deprived districts dominated by public housing, where the improvement of the urban environment and the upgrading of social facilities could have helped to reduce marginality. The objective to stimulate economic development in urban areas, instead, has been approached by programmes such as the Urban Enterprise Zones (Zone Franche Urbane), firstly launched in 1997, and the Urban Renewal and Sustainable Territory Development Programmes (Programmi di Riqualificazione Urbana e Sviluppo Sostenibile del Territorio – 1999), both aimed to stimulate the private sector in contributing to local development and urban regeneration.

The big response by municipalities to these financial opportunities – overall, more than 500 local action plans were approved in around a decade – has meant for hundreds of Italian cities to experience new ways to address urban policy and, in some way, to be prepared when the EU started the Urban Community Initiative. Within the Urban I programme (1994–1999) the EU support went to 16 cities (12 of which in the Southern regions), with actions plans mostly focused on the regeneration of the old towns. The Urban II programme (2000–2006) funded the implementation of further 10 action plans, with a more balanced national distribution and greater attention to the marginal neighborhoods (Figure 1). To give a political response to the high number of

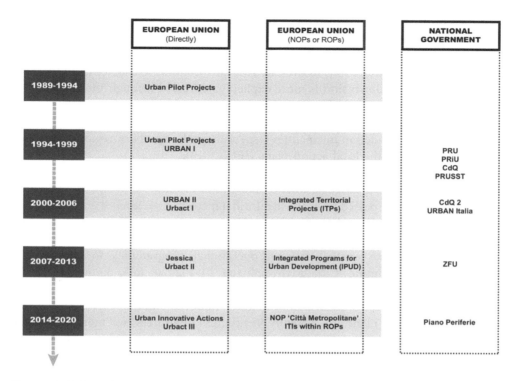

Figure 1. Main urban initiatives promoted by European and National Frameworks in Italy (1989–2020). Source: Author's design.

(unfunded) applications for the Urban II programme, in 2001 the national government decided to allocate around a hundred million euro in a programme (Urban Italia) to partially support the best projects from the cities that were not funded by the EU. The analysis on the effectiveness of the Urban Initiative in Italy is complex (see GHK 2003; Palermo 2002 for the first cycle; ECOTEC 2010 for the second) and provide evidences on the very uneven impact of the programme across the country and over time. For instance, the evaluations suggest the higher impact of the Urban I action plans, which in many cases (notably old towns in Southern cities) were clearly recognized driver for the revitalization processes.

By the mid-2000s, the mainstreaming of the EU approach to Italian urban policy entered into a completely new phase (Vinci 2016), marked by a changed political climate and new balance of power in the management of the EU Structural Funds. Firstly, the State's commitment towards urban issues became extremely rarefied: beyond a second round for the Urban Enterprise Zones (2007), there is nothing comparable to the huge political and financial investment that had characterized the previous decade. Secondly, in the transition between the 2000–2006 and 2007–2013 programming cycles, the implementation of urban initiatives through the Structural Funds were devolved to the complete responsibility of regional authorities.

In the 2000–2006 programming cycle, urban areas are addressed as a thematic dimension within the Integrated Territorial Projects (ITPs), the main planning tool established in the National Strategic Framework to provide a place-based implementation to the Structural Funds. In the only systematic analysis on the implementation of ITPs (Bianchi and Casavola 2009), it is argued that only 18 out of 156 ITPs had an explicit urban focus, amounting to around 15% of the funds available. In the period 2007–2013, the urban dimension is more explicitly addressed through the adoption of Integrated Programmes for Urban Development, to fund area-based action plans in accordance with 'Urban method'. Despite that, however, the few resources available and the high number of funded municipalities (especially in the Southern regions), resulted in a limited impact of the local action plans (IFEL 2013).

After a long silence, cities returned to be a debated issue in national politics on the occasion of a reform of local government passed in 2014: Law 56/2014, also known as the Delrio Reform, was passed to establish a formal metropolitan level of government in the institutional system (Crivello and Staricco 2017). This event is relevant to the urban dimension of EU Cohesion Policy because the government decided to address on metropolitan areas one of the national operational programmes for the period 2014–2020: the programme 'Città Metropolitane 2014–2020' (also known as 'PON Metro') (Vinci 2019). While the Delrio Reform is experiencing huge implementation problems, the PON Metro (worth around nine hundred million euro) has moved forward and 14 action plans are currently in progress to address two main challenges in the metropolitan areas: to increase the efficiency of services to city-users, by promoting a 'smart city' approach, and to face social exclusion through an upgrading of social housing and community facilities in the most deprived neighborhoods.

After two decades of planning experiments across the country, there is no convergence in the domestic debate of whether or not these different types of initiatives can be defined as a national 'urban agenda' in the context of European integration. For instance, starting from the analytical framework provided by other scholars (van Den Berg, Braun, and van der Meer 2007; d'Albergo 2010), Allulli and Tortorella (2013) describe the process to address urban issues by Italian governments as a combination of 'explicit' and 'implicit' national policies, with various 'direct' and 'indirect' effects on the cities' problems. In particular, they argue that these efforts had an extremely limited impact on urban issues for two main reasons: (i) because they cannot be described as a coordinated policy, reflecting sectoral and fragmented political priorities, and (ii) because they represent an incremental adaptation to imperatives and paradigms determined at European level (Allulli and Tortorella 2013, 13). The main obstacles to the emergence of a national urban agenda are therefore identified as follows: on the one hand, in the contested role attributed to municipal authorities after the devolution process started in the nineties, which (paradoxically) were eventually seen by national government as 'policy takers' rather than 'policy makers'; on the other, for the role played by regional government, which – especially after the reform of the title V of the Constitution passed in 2001 (Cammelli 2011) – resulted in increasing tensions between levels of government, a fragmentation of responsibilities, and an overall weakening of the local and urban agendas.

In this context, a special attention has been given in the literature to larger cities. Several works published in recent years (Calafati 2016; Dematteis 2011; Urban@it 2016) do agree on the existence of a clear paradox: while larger Italian cities are home to around one-third of the country's population and represent the place for the main economic processes (Cittalia 2013), they have never been the focus of an explicit national strategy as in other European countries (for instance, France). Consequently, the lack of policy coordination at metropolitan level provides local government with less power to control critical processes for a balanced and sustainable development in urban areas, including sprawl (Balducci, Fedeli, and Curci 2017), environmental conflicts (Secchi 2010), lack of affordable housing (Baldini and Poggio 2014). Policies to face these urban problems, it is argued by more recent analyses (Urban@it 2017), have received clear impulses from the European level, but not enough, however, to foster a lasting political agenda for cities' sustainable development.

3. The Palermo case study

3.1 *A city's overview*

The city of Palermo is the capital and most populated urban area of Sicily, the largest Italian region by territorial extension and the fourth one by number of inhabitants (5 million). With a population of 668,405 inhabitants (2018), it is the fifth city of the country by demographic size, and the core of a functional urban area of around 1 million inhabitants (1.25 million when we consider the metropolitan area established in 2015). As well as many other Italian large cities, over the last three decades, the municipality has experienced a suburbanization process, with a loss of population (of around 6%) towards the mid-sized neighboring towns (Lotta, Picone, and Schilleci 2017). Demographic decline has been poorly compensated by the growth of immigrants, given that such community amounts to only 3.8% of the total population (2017) and is the second smallest among the ten largest Italian cities (Cittalia 2014).

Since the second post-war period, and the enlargement of the bureaucratic structure of regional government, the city's economic profile has been dominated by the public sector. Between the sixties and the eighties, when the urban area underwent considerable expansion, the construction industry – often under Mafia control – also played a central role in the local economy (Morello 2002). Given also the interference the Mafia was able to exert over local government, illegal organizations played a dominating role in affecting urban development during these decades, making this period one of the darkest pages of the modern city's history. It was only by the late nineties, therefore, that other sectors gradually emerged within the local economy, such as tourism and services related to cultural activities (Azzolina 2009).

Any social and economic portrait of the city, however, cannot overlook the clear development gap that still persists compared to the more developed urban areas of Europe and even of the same country. According to the first European Cities Report (EC 2007, EC 2016), in 2001 the value of GDP per capita created in Palermo was the 78% of the EU27 average and the 66% of the Italian average. In the same year the unemployment rate amounted to 29.4%, among the highest rate in the cities surveyed by Urban Audit. In 2016, it still amounted to 21.9%, a value near to double the national average.

From a national perspective, these weaknesses in the city's economic performance need to be considered in light of the development disparities that historically take place between the North and the South of Italy (SVIMEZ 2015). As underlined by other analyses (Urban@it 2019), in fact, after a period of convergence started by the end of the nineties, the crisis had a critical effect in (re)increasing these disparities, not only among northern and southern regions, but also between the major cities located across the country.

The existence of such economic disparities is clearly the effect of a durable vicious circle among several different factors, including a low efficiency of public administration and, therefore, a lack of trust of citizens towards local government. Different surveys, in fact, have reported that citizens are highly unsatisfied with regard to a wide range of policy of critical importance for their quality of life. For instance, EUROSTAT (2016) has revealed that the level of satisfaction for the public transport service and the air quality are the lowest among any of the 79 European cities under analysis. The same source reports that only 22% of people interviewed in Palermo declared themselves satisfied with the state of the streets and buildings in their neighborhood, while many other indicators concerning the perceived quality of housing, education and health facilities relegate the city to the bottom of the European rankings.

Despite this apparent dissatisfaction in local society, from the beginning of the nineties, the city has experienced relatively simple political transitions. In fact, after the turning point given by the national reform of local government in 1993, the city's government has been led by only two mayors directly elected by the citizens: the current mayor Leoluca Orlando (1993–2000, 2012–), supported by a center-left coalition, and Diego Cammarata (2001–2012), supported by a center-right coalition. Given their respective cultural and political backgrounds, the two coalitions provided for an alternative – and sometimes contrasting – view of city's development. As a result, policy-making has been shaped according to different priorities and instruments to combat urban problems and promote local development.

It has been argued (i.e. Azzolina 2009), however, that the two political cycles are also characterized by a certain degree of continuity with respect to a series of development problems experienced by the city, such as, for instance, the need to address the Old Town regeneration. In the following paragraphs and the conclusions, these differences and analogies in addressing city's development will be discussed under the specific perspective of the EU-led urban initiatives.

3.2 *Urban policy in the nineties*

The nineties opened and were marked by trauma resulting in the fatal attacks on the judges Giovanni Falcone and Paolo Borsellino that occurred in 1992. This event represents a turning point in the city's modern history, as it started an unprecedented process of mobilization among the civil society that ended up contaminating local politics. One year later, the first mayor's direct election resulted in the overwhelming victory of Leoluca Orlando, a politician with a proud background as a Mafia fighter (Schneider and Schneider 2003).

As in other Italian Southern cities, such as Naples (Leonardi and Nanetti 2008; Nanetti 2001), the new mayor's mandate has been interpreted as an effort to rebuild civic identity (Bacon and Majeed 2012a). For instance, the main slogan of the election campaign and (later) of the first government decisions was 'a normal city', a way to emphasize the need for a sharp change of direction to remove the factors affecting local government for decades (corruption and inefficiency, first of all), making the city 'abnormal' in its development process. To reach this goal, the mayor surrounded himself – as councilors or to cover strategic positions within government – mainly with representatives of civil society with a high cultural or professional background.

At the early stage of this new political project, the city's renaissance required an improvement of its environmental condition, since the state of decay of many areas had to be considered not only the consequence, but also the reason for illegality, lack of development and social marginality. The strategy adopted by the local government to address this problem was founded on three main policy decisions:

- a new land-use plan, aimed at restoring the lost territorial identity and removing the distortions provided by decades of uncontrolled urban development, mainly led by private and often illegal interests;
- an investment in the city's most deprived neighborhoods, including the marginal public housing estates such as the ZEN, Borgo Nuovo, Brancaccio, but also the Old Town, where social revitalization could have been linked to cultural tourism;
- a more systematic attention to external opportunities – first of all the European projects –, perceived by local government not only as an instrument to finance urban regeneration, but also to innovate local governance and planning practices in the public sector.

While the preparation of the new urban masterplan took around a decade, to the point that it was eventually approved by the subsequent mayor (2002), different renewal projects in the suburban neighborhoods were already started in the mid-nineties: for instance, the municipality managed to receive national funds to start regeneration in Borgo Nuovo and ZEN districts, the most risky and deprived urban areas in the citizens' collective imagination.

However, the clear political 'manifesto' of the city's government for the whole decade was the recovery of the Old Town. By the middle of the last century, the Old Town had lost 80% of its population, from 125,294 inhabitants in 1951 to 24,438 in 1991. As a result of bombing during the second world war, and subsequent collapses in the built-up environment, the area had been abandoned for decades by the former residents and the main commercial activities (Lo Piccolo 1996), to the extent of being identified as a symbol of urban decay in the whole country.

Not surprisingly, when the municipality decided to apply for the Urban I Community Initiative, the choice went to the historic heart of the city, a place where only the integrated approach promoted by the EU would have started a renewal process.

The target area for the action plan, particularly, covered a half of the Old Town (Figure 2 and 3), the two districts bordering the waterfront for an extension of 112 hectares and a population of around 11,000 inhabitants (Vinci 2017). This area reflected the typical problems experienced in the Old Town: high levels of social marginality and unemployment (35%), lack of economic activity, and extremely degraded environment. At the same time, the presence of a lively community and of a huge, often unused, number of historical landmarks paved the way for a culture-led regeneration strategy.

As in other Italian Urban projects (GHK 2003), the physical interventions absorbed a great share of the available budget (54%), often being addressed to the (costly) restoration of buildings for the placement of new cultural facilities, as the flagship

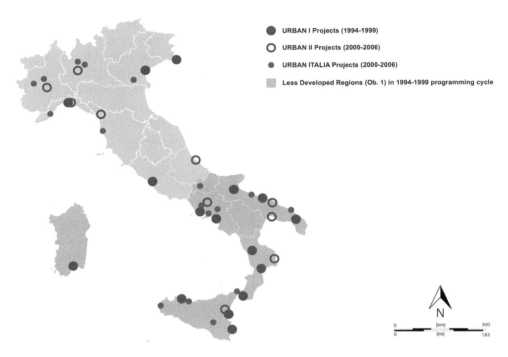

Figure 2. Spatial distribution of the Urban projects in Italy (1994–2006). Source: Author's design.

Figure 3. The Urban I target area within the Old Town. Source: Author's design on satellite view from GoogleMap.

initiative of this type: the recovery of the Spasimo complex, an ancient complex of buildings (including a roofless church) being reconverted into a music and theatre center. Other important interventions regarded the recovery of abandoned public spaces, such for instance the walking over the walls on the waterfront (Mura delle Cattive), that soon became a very popular attraction to citizens and tourists.

The immaterial part of the action plan sought mainly to support activities and services aimed at increasing the neighborhood's attractiveness and reducing social

Figure 4. The two main target areas in the ITP 2000–2006: the Zisa Cultural District (left column) and the former Chimica Arenella (right column), site for the failed Business District project. Source: Author's design on satellite views from GoogleMap (on top); Author's photos (below).

marginalization. For instance, the programme funded small businesses to bring cultural activities in the district (theatre and music labs), to run traditional activities (i.e. handicraft stores), to create new expertise in the field of communication and cultural tourism. Despite the large amount of funds spent on physical interventions, such culture-related measures received in any case significant support, since the action plan budget (20.7 meuro) was greatly co-funded by national, regional and local authorities to integrate the ERDF contribution (40%).

In the systematic analyses available (GHK 2003), the Palermo Urban I project is generally recognized as one of the most successful initiatives within the national panorama. The most important results are identified in the role of the physical interventions as a driver for the regeneration process, and in the success of the culture activities in catalyzing different types of users, helping the district to be rediscovered. Other analyses have underlined the project's contribution to the innovation of urban policy (Tulumello 2016), improving the management capabilities within the municipality or creating the grounds for new governance relations among local stakeholders often not inclined to cooperation (i.e. the conservation authorities). On the contrary, although it is recognized that the project started the Old Town revitalization process, it is argued in another analysis (Palermo 2002) that it was unable to contaminate other critical dimensions for urban regeneration, including the quality of housing or the increase of basic services to residents.

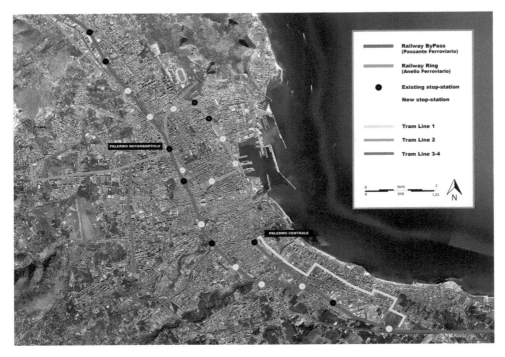

Figure 5. Interventions on the rail network funded in the 2007–2013 programming cycle. Source: Author's design on satellite view from GoogleMap.

3.3 *The 2000s and the challenge to widen the scale and scope of planning*

In Section 2 we argued that in the period 2000–2006, the support for urban development in Italy is characterized by a certain degree of uncertainty. In fact, while urban areas are identified as a priority within the National Strategic Framework (Priority 5 'Cities'), on the other side regions were left free to decide how to deal with the urban dimension and whether to combine it with other development priorities within the Integrated Territorial Projects (ITPs). Therefore, in many Southern Italian regions (including Sicily) the ITPs were conceived as multisectoral programmes, focused on a wide range of development priorities and often on unclear territorial targets.

In the city of Palermo, this new planning challenge falls within a critical change in the local politics. After two consecutive elections won by the center-left, in 2001 local government went to a center-right coalition headed by Diego Cammarata, a mayor belonging to the party (Forza Italia) that in the same year dominated the national elections. It has been argued that this change in the city's political leadership cannot be understood simply as an administrative turnover, but also as a broader change in the perception of the city's identity and on the political discourse around local development (Azzolina 2009; Vinci 2017). The rhetoric of the 'normal city', for instance, had been replaced by new political slogans claiming for a renewed role of the city in the international marketplace, a development perspective that would have required a modernization process of the city's infrastructures and the creation of more advanced services to attract new companies. This transition was accompanied also by a sharp

Figure 6. The Tram Line 1 crossing the Brancaccio neighborhood. Source: Maria Lieta Chiara.

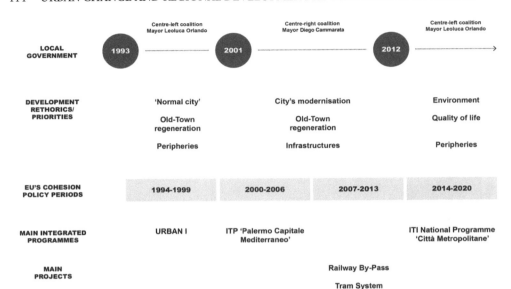

Figure 7. Political cycles and planning priorities in the local government from the 1990s onward. Source: Author's design.

change in the style of government, since in contrast to the approach adopted by the previous mayor (Bacon and Majeed 2012b), key planning responsibilities were placed in the hands of external experts.

These new priorities were translated into a series of planning initiatives undertaken by the new city's government in the early 2000s: (a) an integrated plan for the redevelopment of the public transport system, whose implementation took place many years later (see next section) and (b) the Integrated Territorial Project 'Palermo Capitale dell'Euro-Mediterraneo' (Palermo. Capital of Euro-Mediterranean) in the framework of the 2000–2006 EU Cohesion Policy.

This last, in particular, followed the idea that the city could have played a greater role in the Mediterranean area, as it had for many centuries in the past. Furthermore, since in those years the EU was deciding where to allocate a series of headquarters for the Euro-Mediterranean partnership, the ITP seemed to be the proper response to create what the city was missing in that competition (Comune di Palermo 2002).

With this strategy as the backdrop, shared with a wide partnership – including the Province, the University, the Chamber of Commerce and the Agency for Tourism –, the ITP provided for an ambitious action plan, worth around 100 million euro, structured around two main thematic objectives: supporting the city's identity as a cluster for the Euro-Mediterranean culture; creating a more innovative economic environment, to make the city more attractive to business in the Mediterranean area. These goals were pursued by means of a set of projects and actions of different kinds (physical infrastructures, aids to enterprises, research and training schemes), following the idea of ensuring their functional integration into three main-targeted areas: the Old Town, three former industrial complexes (two of which abandoned since the beginning of XX century), and the University campus.

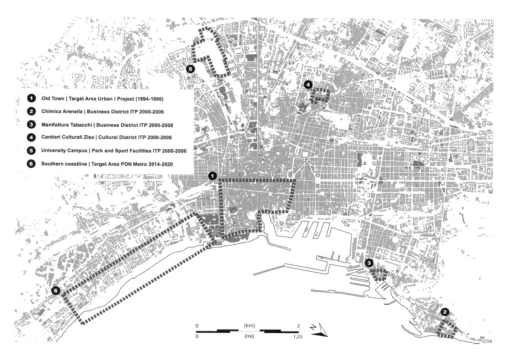

Figure 8. Spatial distribution of the areas targeted by the urban-integrated projects. Source: Author's design.

Within the Old Town, the project tried to provide continuity to the regeneration process started by the Urban programme. After an unsuccessful application to the Urban II Community Initiative with an action plan targeted on the part of the district uncovered by the Urban I project, the ITP aimed to further strengthen the identity of the Old Town as a tourist destination: the main projects undertaken were the recovering of a series of open spaces and green areas and, among the immaterial actions, measures to provide financial support to the small retailers in the traditional markets. The goal of strengthening the city's cultural identity was translated into a series of projects to create new facilities and museums related to the Euro-Mediterranean concept. The flagship project in this field was a new museum of contemporary art, a massive intervention (9 million euro) in the Cantieri Culturali alla Zisa, an ancient industrial site partially reconverted into a cultural district at the end of the nineties (Figure 4). Other cultural facilities were located into the Old Town as part of a cultural itinerary including theatres and historical buildings.

The goal to innovate the city's economic profile was mainly based on the creation of two new business parks to be located within the Chimica Arenella (Figure 4) and the Manifattura Tabacchi, abandoned factories at the northern edge of the harbor area. These facilities would have worked both as business incubators and exhibition areas, to attract the high-tech sector and enable new companies to find their way into the emerging markets. To this aim, these physical interventions were accompanied by several training programmes (partly developed by the University) to create a business culture among the younger generations and those starting up the incubators.

The ITP's implementation has proved to be extremely complex and full of obstacles from the start. Despite the fact that the action plan has been revised several times, some of the largest projects were abandoned, including the two business parks upon which the economic strategy of the whole-integrated project was based. According to an ex-post evaluation of the ITP (Vinci 2009), renovation costs for the business parks projects were largely underestimated, as well as the willingness of the local business sector to support such a complex initiative. Problems of implementation also affected the part of the integrated project focused on culture and tourism, with the consequence of downsizing its impact over the whole planning strategy. For instance, the access to financial incentives from small enterprises in the Old Town was extremely rare, as were in general all the measures to stimulate the birth of new activities in the cultural sector (Vinci 2009).

In the light of these problems, the project's main impact must be limited to pursuing a culture-led regeneration process on the pathway tracked by previous planning experiences. For instance, the project has clearly continued the physical regeneration of the Old Town (as the Urban I initiative started to do a few years before), as well as supporting the development of the ZISA cultural district, despite the implementation issues experienced for the creation of the new Euro-Mediterranean museum. On the contrary, the ITP 2000–2006 has failed in affecting the economic profile of the city in the long term, as greatly emphasized within the project's strategy. In fact, despite a promising project partnership, the project implementation revealed clear weaknesses in the local economic environment, or at least a misleading evaluation by policy-makers on the role the city could have played within the international marketplace.

3.4 *The late 2000s and the transition from the pre- to the post-crisis urban policies*

While the municipality was committed to starting the ITP implementation, local government launched the largest infrastructure scheme ever planned since the post-war reconstruction: the 'Integrated Plan for Mass Public Transport' (PMPT). This programme, approved in 2002 to reshape the urban rail network, can be seen a response to the city's modernization process claimed by the new center-right coalition and, on the other hand, an attempt to provide citizens with an alternative to the car-dependent development pattern characterizing the city's modern history (Vinci and Di Dio 2016).

Despite being a comprehensive strategy for the public transit system, the PMTP combined both new and previously planned projects, part of which under the responsibility of the national rail operator (RFI). Particularly, the plan provided for the following four main interventions over the urban rail network (Figure 5): (1) the redevelopment of around 30 kilometers of the existing rail lines running through the metropolitan area, from the South-Eastern neighborhoods to the airport (Rail By-Pass); (2) the extension of an existing urban rail to serve the city and to connect it to the main rail stations (Rail Ring); (3) three tram lines (Tram Network) to ensure faster connections to remote (and decayed) neighborhoods in the Western and Southern sides of the urban area (Figure 6); (4) a project for a new subway line running from the North to the South of the city.

For the huge costs required for the plan implementation, this last project was soon suspended, while the remaining interventions had to wait 2007 before being started. The projects on the rail network and the tram system, instead, received extensive support from the EU Structural Funds, to the point that the 'Rail By-Pass' (Passante Ferroviario) is one of the largest projects ever co-funded by the EU in the Italian cities (around 1,1 billion euro). The completion of this last project, however, has been slowed down by a series of implementation issues, including rising construction costs and geological problems that to date are still limiting its full efficiency. At the same time, implementation issues are also affecting the other project on the urban rail network (Rail Ring), which, due to the financial problems of the company responsible for the construction, is expected to enter in service not before 2023. The Tram Network (opened in 2015), therefore, is the only fully completed project among those planned in 2002.

Despite such clear implementation problems, however, these projects had the effect of creating new and shared perceptions on what the city would have required to become more 'liveable' and developed. In fact, when in 2012 the city's political leadership turned back to the center-left coalition, mayor Orlando declared that sustainable mobility would take a central place also in his government's activity. The first initiatives undertaken in this field eventually included both low-cost projects, such as the pedestrianization of small areas within the Old Town, but also an ambitious project (currently under development) to double the Tram Network bringing the tracks within the city centre.

While these sectoral policies have systematically benefited from EU funding, the 2007–2013 programming cycle is without a doubt the least significant period for the area-based approach to urban policy. In the few systematic works available on this period (see for instance IFEL 2013), it is underlined that the urban initiatives related to EU funds were negatively affected by many factors, including the few resources available and the decisions taken by regions during implementation. In Sicily, for instance, regional government allowed access to the ERDF 'urban priority' to all cities with a population of at least 30,000 inhabitants, which meant 26 action plans. Such a distributive approach ended up reducing the critical mass of the urban programmes, penalizing the larger cities. Moreover, the complexity of the procedures to evaluate the projects submitted by the municipalities in most cases had the result of slowing down implementation, to the point that funds were lost for hundreds of operations (Tulumello 2016).

In this context, the decision taken by the city of Palermo for its urban initiative has increased complexity, creating the conditions for the poor results achieved after implementation. The integrated project submitted by the municipality was an explicit continuation of the ITP 2000–2006, from which it took a similar name (Palermo. Capital City), the strategy to improve the city's international profile, its focus over the areas where previously it was expected the creation of the cultural district (Cantieri Culturali alla Zisa) and the business district (Chimica Arenella). The implementation of this last, however, failed again and due to the highly bureaucratized procedures established by the Region, other operations were replaced or even abandoned. As a consequence, the programme – in its final version worth less than 10 million euro – took the form of a list of small and disconnected interventions with no significant impact on local development.

The poor results achieved by the urban programme in the 2007–2013 period are the consequence of different variables, not entirely connected to local factors. In a report (IFEL 2013), it is argued that urban programmes were affected by the altered direction of national government, which at first had granted a large degree of autonomy to the regional authorities, eventually replaced by centralized mechanisms when they seemed unable to make an effective use of funding. In this context of uncertainty, as in other circumstances in the past, the Sicily regional government lacked to provide any clear strategy for urban development with the consequence to adopt no selective mechanism to transfer the funds to cities. As a result, in the austerity climate that was affecting local government (Dematteis 2011; Urban@it 2017), the urban programmes were merely understood to be subsidies to deal with routine interventions and the case of Palermo makes no exception.

3.5 New solutions to old strategies: dealing with the urban priorities in 2014-2020 programming cycle

In recent years, it has been underlined in many works (Bachtler et al. 2017; McCann 2015; Piattoni and Polverari 2016) that the years across the 2007–2013 and 2014–2020 funding periods represent not only a simple passage between two programming cycles, but a more radical redefinition of the principles, aims and mechanism to ensure a territorial dimension to Cohesion Policy. Clear indications in this respect can be found in the way sustainable urban development was treated within the ERDF regulation approved in 2013, and also if we look at the content of the thematic priorities for the 'urban agenda' the EU is trying to put in place after the Pact of Amsterdam (Atkinson and Zimmermann 2016).

Given the context examined in Section 2, this process has implied some additional challenges for Italian cities: (a) the need to for the municipalities to rapidly adapt their urban agendas to a series of new (and often unexplored) issues for policy-making, including intermunicipal cooperation, and (b) to translate into a planning perspective a response to some (unsolved) socio-economic consequences of the crisis. The clearest example where to find both these questions is the already mentioned PON Metro, the programme the Italian government launched in 2014 to address the EU urban agenda on metropolitan areas.

Considering the strict planning framework of the national programme, the overall objectives of the city of Palermo are not radically different from other cities. They are mostly (1) supporting metropolitan government, through ICT solutions shared with the 82 municipalities of the metropolitan area, (2) increasing the efficiency of the services provided to citizens and city-users, with a greater focus on sustainable mobility and public transport, and (c) fighting social exclusion, through the creation of new facilities, services and housing opportunities to the disadvantaged groups primarily in the marginal neighborhoods.

The local action plan, approved in 2017 and funded with 91.9 million euro, is based on a high number of very different projects (48), ranging from physical interventions such as those to secure energy efficiency in the urban infrastructures to a series of immaterial measures to fight urban poverty, such as, for instance the creation of a new agency to facilitate access to social housing. Despite such heterogeneity, however, around two-thirds of the budget for the action plan has been allocated to the 'smart city' component of the development strategy. Just to give an example, around 20 million euros are being invested to modernize and make more efficient the urban lighting system, while the implementation of the ICT platforms to support metropolitan government will draw a remaining 18% of the budget (16 million euros). Although the project implementation is still in progress, the method for the funds allocation provides interesting evidence on the way the urban dimension is being treated within the current programming cycle. On the one hand, despite the overall strategy of the programme was to address the metropolitan dimension, as a result of a national decision to minimize the implementation problems, 80% of funds will be concentrated in the core city. Secondly, although there is a claim for an area-based approach, the largest part of the measures aimed at reducing social marginality are not so clearly spatially concentrated: for instance, in order to secure funding for the projects with low risks of failure, the measures towards social marginality were spread by the municipality over different neighborhoods.

In light of these planning decisions, the PON Metro action plan can be described as the attempt to give different (and to some extent more advanced) responses to the development priorities already pursued by the city. A clear example in this respect is the strategy to enhance sustainable mobility, which has remained a topical question for local government during the whole last decade. After the 2007–2013 period had secured considerable investments on the transport infrastructures in the city, the planning focus in the PON Metro seems to have been shifted to the 'soft' elements of sustainable mobility: for instance, around 20% of the project budget (18 million euros) has been allocated for a package including the renovation of the buses fleet, a complete remote control of public transport, and further development of the shared mobility systems.

These efforts towards sustainable mobility will be further supported through the funds the city will receive under the so-called 'regional urban agenda', the part of the ERDF Operational Programme the Sicily region has addressed to its main urban areas. Furthermore, in April 2017 the mayor announced he had reached an agreement ('Patto per Palermo') with national government for a multiannual financial framework, the largest part of which will be spent to double the current Tram network. These last developments make it clear not only that sustainable mobility is likely to be the main driver for urban change in the near future, but also the area where, in the long run, the EU Cohesion Policy has made the most recognizable impact on the urban development process.

4. Which legacy in the long term? final remarks

In the twenty years, since the Urban Community Initiative made its appearance in Palermo, many changes have taken place in the city's development process. In the long run, therefore, one may find the existence of a clearer element of continuity across the EU programming cycles, as well as marked changes in direction in the way the problem of sustainable urban development has been perceived by policy-makers and the EU funds employed for such purpose (Figure 7).

According to some works (i.e Azzolina 2009), a clear element of continuity in policy-making since the mid of the nineties can be found in the focus on physical regeneration and the support for a culture-led development process. In other works (i.e Vinci and Di Dio 2016), it is argued that another common thread across the years (and the political coalitions) can be found in the attention towards sustainable mobility, despite the fact that the creation of massive transport infrastructures has been gradually added to by smaller and less costly interventions, such as, for instance, car-free areas, pedestrianization projects, and the application of 'smart' solutions to the existing mobility systems.

Concerning these two issues, the case study shows that the planning initiatives deriving from the EU Cohesion Policy have played an important role in different directions. First, by providing funding to successful projects that probably would not have been implemented without the EU support (i.e. projects on the rail network). Secondly, stimulating the municipality to apply new methods in policy-making: for instance, an integrated approach to urban regeneration after the Urban initiative or, more recently, a smart city approach to urban sustainability through the PON Metro.

At the same time, in the last twenty years we find clear changes of direction in the way the EU instruments and funding opportunities have been embedded in the local policy-making. This discontinuity has to be related both to 'external' and 'internal' factors. For the external factors, we mainly refer to the changed priorities and mechanism that European, national and regional authorities have established, from one period to another (see Section 1), to address urban development through the Structural Funds. As regard the internal factors, the case study seeks to show that, despite the fact that, from the nineties onward, local government has experienced relatively simple political transitions, some different views on city's development ended up affecting the implementation of many urban initiatives under the umbrella of the EU (see Subsections 3.2 and 3.3).

An interesting perspective to understand how these factors (internal and external ones) may have an impact on the policy-making process related to the EU programmes is rendered by the way action plans have been territorialized within the urban area (Figure 8). In the nineties, when the local government priority was the Old Town regeneration, the Urban initiative was targeted on a very small part of a single neighborhood (1,1 square miles). In the following period (2000–2006), when no guidelines for spatial concentration were given to municipalities and local government wished to increase the city's competitiveness, the target of the EU projects became the whole urban area. This process has continued until the current programming cycle, when the action plan of the PON Metro includes measures to stimulate effects even at the metropolitan scale. We can draw two main lessons from this changing approach: first, that the area-based initiatives (Andersson and Musterd 2005) or the tension towards the neighborhood (Atkinson 2008) have been increasingly replaced by other forms of spatiality respect to which the aim of planning integration is more controversial; secondly, that territorial concentration seems to have favored the projects' effectiveness, since the smaller project for spatial dimension (Urban) is the only that have been successfully implemented.

The discontinuity in the aims, territorial targets, and outcomes of the examined planning initiatives does not make it a simple task to figure out their effectiveness and an even harder one to find evidence from a comparative analysis. However, it can be argued that in certain circumstances the city's development process has been clearly influenced by the EU projects, and their legacy has to be found both in the 'direct' and in a series of 'indirect' effects on policy-making. Turning back to the research questions outlined in the introduction, these effects can be explained as follows.

With regards to the impact on the city's development process (RQ1), the clearest effect of the implemented integrated projects can be perceived in the contribution to the Old Town regeneration. In the whole of Section 3, it is underlined how the recovering of this ruined part of the city has been a concern of local government since the early nineties. As the regeneration process is the result of a series of interconnected policies undertaken by the municipality (i.e. incentives to housing renovation), isolating the effects provided by the projects funded by the EU is not easy. In line with previous works (Azzolina 2009; GHK 2003; Palermo 2002), however, it can be argued that the Urban initiative represents a milestone in the Old Town regeneration for the double effect to have (a) recovered buildings and public spaces (often reconverted into cultural facilities) that became epicenters for the district revitalization and (b) for having started to reverse its negative reputation, stimulating the coming back of residents and commercial activities. The impact of other initiatives on urban regeneration has proved to be generally poor. The ITP 2000-2006 – the most ambitious in terms of development strategy and funds available – has failed to follow up the revitalization process in the Old Town and even more limited were their outcomes in the other targeted areas.

In the last few years, the city is undergoing a 'mobility revolution' that is expected to critically change the quality of life in the urban area. Here the EU programming has been playing a crucial role for two main reasons: more simply in terms of funding, as the largest transport infrastructures implemented over the last decade were strongly supported by Structural Funds, but also in stimulating different ways of thinking to mobility planning and management, integrating conventional and innovative approaches, 'hard' and 'soft' intervention in the mobility domain (see also comments on RQ3).

Concerning the influence of the European projects on local governance (RQ2), this question has been approached from two main perspectives: in terms of cooperation among public authorities and of public–private partnership within the integrated projects. With regard to the first type of cooperation, all the examined planning initiatives were promoted by the municipality with the involvement of public authorities/stakeholders performing different roles during the projects' design and implementation. In the Urban project, for instance, all the interventions on historical buildings were agreed with – and supervised by – the local authority for the protection of cultural heritage (Soprintendenza). In the following ITP (2000–2006), a major role was played by the University, having been a pillar of the project strategy and a beneficiary of several measures, including support to research and training activities and funds for the improvement of sport facilities within its main campus. More recently (2014–2020), a novel form of public–public partnership is related to the PON Metro implementation, since some measures to strengthen metropolitan government have required a close cooperation between the city of Palermo (as the leading authority of the project) and the 82 municipalities of the metropolitan area. Although such collaborations were driven by the priorities of each project (and often formally required), we can argue the EU initiatives have constantly encouraged a dialogue among the main local public stakeholders.

The opinion on the role of public–private partnership over time, instead, is much more controversial. During the nineties, in the climate of openness to civil society promoted by the major Orlando (Bacon and Majeed 2012a), cultural organizations had a leading role in the design of the Urban I action plan, alongside wide implementation responsibilities for some successful projects. We find a dialogue with local associations also in the different integrated projects that, from 2000 to 2013, tried to support the creation of a cultural district in the ZISA complex.

On the contrary, the involvement of the business community has generally led to results that are far from expectations. Much evidence suggests (Vinci 2009) that the clearest failure lies in ITP 2000–2006, the most ambitious public–private partnership cooperation ever conceived in the framework of the EU projects. After the projects for the two business districts were abandoned, a large part of the incentives that the municipality had agreed with the Chamber of Commerce and other private stakeholders ended up being revoked. Even in the Old Town, where the regeneration process was encouraging private investments, the project to revitalize the traditional markets failed due to the contrasts with the small local retailers. After such a troubled experience, the EU initiatives have generally assigned more limited implementation responsibilities to the private sector, beyond 'formal' consultations in the early stages of the planning processes.

Also, because of these issues, the planning initiatives in the framework of the EU programming are generally designed and implemented with a dominating role of the municipality. This makes any critical discussion around planning innovation (RQ3) closely related to the city's administrative structure, its organization, and approach to public policy over time. From this perspective, the period in the nineties after mayor Orlando came into office is seen as a period of drastic change (Bacon and Majeed 2012b). The growing opportunities deriving from the EU Cohesion Policy have clearly encouraged an innovation process within the municipality, to the extent that the need to secure an effective implementation to the Urban initiative led to the creation of a special unit that took broader responsibilities for the European projects (Azzolina 2009). This department has proved to be of key importance for policy-making much beyond the Urban experience: for instance, in disseminating a new planning culture among the city's various departments or, not least by creating new technical skills within the municipality.

Such capacity building process, however, cannot be defined as coherent or continuous over time. In the 2000s, when planning responsibilities were increasingly outsourced to external experts, the unit devoted to the EU projects was partly dismantled. Although no direct correlation can be found with the poor performance of the EU projects in that period, it can be argued that the lack of clear management responsibilities within the municipality didn't help implementation.

In the last decade, the municipality has shown great ability in catalyzing funds for large projects which otherwise would have not been secured by other sources. As a result, since large transport projects started to be seen as the driving force for the city's renovation, the department for infrastructures has gradually taken a bigger role within the city's organization. For instance, by taking critical implementation responsibilities in the PON Metro project (2014–2020) and the leadership of the planning process to update the sustainable urban mobility plan (SUMP), an instrument that generally requires a strong collaborative approach within and outside the municipality. In the long-term perspective, it is adopted in this work, this re-balancing of powers within the municipality reflects a broader political process that might have serious implications for the future perspectives of sustainable urban development: there is evidence, in fact, that t the administrative structure is gradually adapting itself to the only priorities that give (or have given) local government greater guarantees to succeed. In other words, no cultural and technical investment is being made on policy-making innovation to meet the future challenge of an EU-led urban agenda.

Disclosure statement

No potential conflict of interest was reported by the author.

ORCID

Ignazio Vinci http://orcid.org/0000-0003-3927-8432

References

Allulli, M., and W. Tortorella. 2013. "Cities in Search of Policy. The Urban Issue in the Italian National Political Agenda." *Métropoles* 12: 1–18. Accessed 8 January 2019. http://metropoles.revues.org/4654

Andersson, R., and S. Musterd. 2005. "Area-based Policies: A Critical Appraisal." *Tijdschrift Voor Economische En Sociale Geografie* 96 (4): 377–389. doi:10.1111/j.1467-9663.2005.00470.x.

Artioli, F. 2016. "Cities in the Italian Political System: Incomplete Actors and Objects of Policies." In *Cities as Political Objects. Historical Evolution, Analytical Categorisations and Institutional Challenges of Metropolitanisation*, edited by A. Cole and R. Payre, 135–155. Cheltenham: Edward Elgar Publishing.

Atkinson, R. 2008. "European Urban Policies and the Neighbourhood: An Overview." *Urban Design and Planning* 161(3): 115–122. doi: 10.1680/udap.2008.161.3.115.

Atkinson, R. 2015. "The Urban Dimension in Cohesion Policy: Past Development and Future Perspective." *European Structural and Investment Funds Journal* 3 (1): 21–31. https://estif.lexxion.eu/article/ESTIF/2015/1/5

Atkinson, R., and K. Zimmermann. 2016. "Cohesion Policy and Cities: An Ambivalent Relationship?" In *Handbook on Cohesion Policy in the EU*, edited by S. Piattoni and L. Polverari, 413–426. Cheltenham: Edward Elgar.

Avarello, P., and M. Ricci, eds. 2000. *Politiche Urbane. Dai Programmi Complessi alle Politiche Integrate di Sviluppo Urbano*. Roma: INU Edizioni.

Azzolina, L. 2009. *Governare Palermo. Storia e Sociologia di un Cambiamento Mancato*. Rome: Donzelli.

Bachtler, J., P. Berkowitz, S. Hardy, and T. Muravska, eds. 2017. *EU Cohesion Policy: Reassising Performance and Directions*. London-New York: Routledge.

Bacon, L., and R. Majeed. 2012a. "Palermo Renaissance Part 1: Rebuilding Civic Identity and Reclaiming a City from the Mafia in Italy, 1993-2000." *Innovations for Successful Societies*, Princeton University. Paper. https://successfulsocieties.princeton.edu/publications/palermo-renaissance-part-1-rebuilding-civic-identity-and-reclaiming-city-mafia-italy

Bacon, L., and R. Majeed. 2012b. "Palermo Renaissance Part 2: Reforming City Hall, 1993-2000." *Innovations for Successful Societies*, Princeton University. Paper. https://successfulsocieties.princeton.edu/publications/palermo-renaissance-part-2-reforming-city-hall-1993-2000

Baldini, M., and T. Poggio. 2014. "The Italian Housing System and the Global Financial Crisis." *Journal of Housing and the Built Environment* 29: 317–334. doi:10.1007/s10901-013-9389-7.

Balducci, A., V. Fedeli, and F. Curci, eds. 2017. *Post-Metropolitan Territories and Urban Space*. London-New York: Routledge.

Bianchi, T., and P. Casavola. 2009. "Integrated Territorial Projects in the 2000-2006 CSF - Objective 1. Theories, Evidence and Views on Local Development Policy." Materiali UVAL. 17. Rome. http://old2018.agenziacoesione.gov.it/opencms/export/sites/dps/it/documentazione/servizi/materiali_uval/analisi_e_studi/Muval_17_eng.pdf

Calafati, A. 2016. "The Metropolitan Question in Italy." *Rivista Italiana di Economia, Demografia e Statistica* 70 (2): 15–34. http://dx.doi.org/10.2139/ssrn.2877313

Cammelli, M. 2011. "Governo delle Città: Profili Istituzionali." In *Le Grandi Città Italiane: Società e Territori da Ricomporre*, edited by G. Dematteis, 335–378. Venice: Marsilio.

Carpenter, J. 2013. "Sustainable Urban Regeneration within the European Union: A Case of 'Europeanization'." In *The Routledge Companion to Urban Regeneration*, edited by M. E. Leary and J. McCarthy, 138–147. London-New York: Routledge.

Cittalia. 2013. *Le Città Metropolitane*. Rome: Fondazione Anci Ricerche.

Cittalia. 2014. *Taccuino Metropolitano*. Rome: Fondazione Anci Ricerche.

Comune di Palermo. 2002. *Progetto Integrato Territoriale Palermo Capitale dell'Euromediterraneo*. Mimeo. Palermo.

Cremaschi, M. 2003. *Progetti di Sviluppo del Territorio. Le Azioni Integrate in Italia e in Europa*. Milan: Il Sole 24 Ore.

Crivello, S., and L. Staricco. 2017. "Institutionalizing Metropolitan Cities in Italy. Success and Limits of a Centralistic, Simplifying Approach." *Urban Research & Practice* 10 (2): 228–238. doi:10.1080/17535069.2017.1307001.

d'Albergo, E. 2010. "Urban Issues in Nation-State Agendas: A Comparison in Western Europe." *Urban Research & Practice* 3 (2): 138–158. doi:10.1080/17535069.2010.481220.

Dematteis, G., ed. 2011. *Le Grandi Città Italiane: Società e Territori da Ricomporre*. Venice: Marsilio.

Dossi, S. 2017. *Cities and the European Union. Mechanisms and Modes of Europeanisation*. London: Rowman & Littlefield International.

EC – European Commission. 1997. *Towards an Urban Agenda in the European Union. Communication from the Commission to the Council and Parliament*. Bruxelles: European Commission.

EC – European Commission. 1998. *Sustainable Urban Development in the European Union: A Framework for Action. Communication from the Commission to the Council and Parliament*. Bruxelles: European Commission.

EC – European Commission. 2007. *State of European Cities Report*. Luxembourg: Office for Official Publications of the European Communities.

EC – European Commission. 2008. *Fostering the Urban Dimension: Analysis of the Operational Programmes Co-financed by the European Regional Development Fund (2007-2013)*. Luxembourg: Office for Official Publications of the European Communities.

EC – European Commission. 2009. *Promoting Sustainable Urban Development in Europe: Achievements and Opportunities*. Luxembourg: Office for Official Publications of the European Communities.

ECOTEC. 2010. *Ex-Post Evaluation of Cohesion Policy Programmes 2000-06: The URBAN Community Initiative*.Final Report to the European Commission. Bruxelles: DG Regio.

EC – European Commission. 2011a. *The Urban and Regional Dimension of Europe 2020: Seventh Progress Report on Economic, Social and Territorial Cohesion*. Luxembourg: Publications Office of the European Union.

EC – European Commission. 2011b. *Cities of Tomorrow Challenges: Visions, Ways Forward*. Luxembourg: Publications Office of the European Union.

EC – European Commission. 2014a. *Investment for Jobs and Growth: Promoting Development and Good Governance in EU Regions and Cities. Sixth Report on Economic, Social and territorial cohesion*. Luxembourg: Publications Office of the European Union.

EC – European Commission. 2014b. *The Urban Dimension of EU Policies: Key Features of an EU Urban Agenda. Communication from the Commission to the Council and Parliament*. Bruxelles: European Commission.
EC – European Commission. 2016. *State of European Cities Report*. Luxembourg: Office for Official Publications of the European Communities.EP.
ECORYS. 2010. "The Urban Dimension of the ERDF in the 2007-2013 Period: Implementation and Practice in Five European Cities." Report for the European Commission. Bruxelles.
EP – European Parliament. 2005. *Report on the Urban Dimension in the Context of Enlargement*. Bruxelles: European Parliament.
EP – European Parliament. 2014. *The Role of Cities in Cohesion Policy*. Bruxelles: European Parliament.
EUROSTAT. 2016. *Urban Europe. Statistics on Cities, Towns and Suburbs*. Luxembourg: European Union.
GHK. 2003. "Ex-post Evaluation Urban Community Initiative (1994-1999)." *Final Report*.
Governa, F., and C. Salone. 2005. "Italy and European Spatial Policies: Polycentrism, Urban Networks and Local Innovation Practices." *European Planning Studies* 13 (2): 265–283. doi:10.1080/0965431042000321820.
Hamedinger, A., and A. Wolffhardt. 2010. *The Europeanization of Cities: Policies, Urban Change and Urban Networks*. Amsterdam: Techne Press.
IFEL. 2013. *La Dimensione Territoriale nel Quadro Strategico Nazionale 2007-2013*. Rome: Fondazione Anci Ricerche.
Janin Rivolin, U. 2003. "Shaping European Spatial Planning: How Italy's Experience Can Contribute." *Town Planning Review* 74 (1): 51–76. doi:10.3828/tpr.74.1.4.
Leonardi, R. 2005. *Cohesion Policy in the European Union*. Basingstoke: Palgrave Macmillan.
Leonardi, R., and R. Y. Nanetti. 2008. *La Sfida di Napoli. Capitale Sociale, Sviluppo e Sicurezza*. Milan: Guerini.
Lo Piccolo, F. 1996. "Urban Renewal in the Historic Centre of Palermo." *Planning Practice & Research* 11 (2): 217–226. doi:10.1080/02697459650036369.
Lotta, F., M. Picone, and F. Schilleci. 2017. "Palermo. An Incomplete Post-metropolitan Area." In *Post-Metropolitan Territories and Urban Space*, edited by A. Balducci, V. Fedeli, and F. Curci, 161–182. London-New York: Routledge.
Matkó, M. 2016. "Sustainable Urban Development in Cohesion Policy Programmes 2014-2020, a Brief Overview". Paper presented at *Urban Development Network Meeting*, 18 February 2016, Bruxelles.
McCann, P. 2015. *The Regional and Urban Policy of the European Union*. Cheltenham: Elgar Publishing.
Medeiros, E., ed. 2019. *Territorial Cohesion. The Urban Dimension*. Berlin-Heidelberg: Springer.
Medeiros, E. A., and Z. van der. 2019. "Evaluating Integrated Sustainable Urban Development Strategies: A Methodological Framework Applied in Portugal." *European Planning Studies*. doi:10.1080/09654313.2019.1606898.
Morello, M. 2002. *Organizzazione, Piano e Governo Urbano. A Partire da Palermo*. Milan: Franco Angeli.
Nanetti, R. Y. 2001. "Adding Value to City Planning: The European Union's Urban Programs in Naples." *South European Society and Politics* 6 (3): 33–57. doi:10.1080/714004954.
Olsen, J. 2002. "The Many Faces of Europeanization." *Journal of Common Market Studies* 40 (5): 921–952. doi:10.1111/1468-5965.00403.
Ombuen, S., M. Ricci, and O. Segnalini, eds. 2000. *I Programmi Complessi. Innovazione e Piano nell'Europa delle Regioni*. Milan: Il Sole 24 Ore.
Palermo, P. C., ed. 2002. *Il Programma Urban e l'Innovazione delle Politiche Urbane*, 1–3. Milan: Franco Angeli.
Parkinson, M. 2006. "Cohesion Policy and Cities in Europe." *Inforegio Panorama* 19: 7–10.
Pasqui, G. 2005. *Territori: Progettare lo Sviluppo. Teorie, Strumenti, Esperienze*. Rome: Carocci.
Piattoni, S., and L. Polverari, eds. 2016. *Handbook on Cohesion Policy in the EU*. Cheltenham: Edward Elgar Publishing.

Radaelli, C. M. 2003. "The Europeanization of Public Policy." In *The Politics of Europeanization*, edited by K. Featherstone and C. M. Radaelli, 27–56. Oxford: Oxford University Press.

Ramsden, P., and L. Colini 2013. *"Urban Development in the EU: 50 Projects Supported by the European Regional Development Fund during the 2007-13 Period."* Final Report to the European Commission. Luxembourg: Publications Office of the European Union.

Schneider, P. T., and J. Schneider. 2003. *Reversible Destiny: Mafia, Antimafia, and the Struggle for Palermo*. Berkeley and Los Angeles: University of California Press.

Secchi, B. 2010. "A New Urban Question." *Territorio* 53: 8–18. doi:10.3280/TR2010-053002.

SVIMEZ. 2015. *Rapporto sull'Economia Del Mezzogiorno*. Bologna: il Mulino.

Tulumello, S. 2016. "Multi-level Territorial Governance and Cohesion Policy. Structural Funds and the Timing of Development in Palermo and the Italian Mezzogiorno." *European Journal of Spatial Development* 62: 1–23.

Urban@it. 2016. *Rapporto sulle Città. Metropoli Attraverso La Crisi*. Bologna: il Mulino.

Urban@it. 2017. *Secondo Rapporto sulle Città. Le Agende Urbane delle Città Italiane*. Bologna: il Mulino.

Urban@it. 2019. *Il Governo Debole delle Economie Urbane*. Bologna: il Mulino.

van Den Berg, L., J. Braun, and J. van der Meer, eds. 2007. *National Policy Responses to Urban Challenges in Europe*. Aldershot: Ashgate.

van der Zwet, A., J. Bachtler, M. Ferry, I. McMaster, and S. Miller 2017. "Integrated Territorial and Urban Strategies: How are ESIF Adding Value in 2014-2020?" Final Report, Directorate-General for Regional and Urban Policy, European Commission.

Vandelli, L. 2000. *Il Governo Locale*. Bologna: il Mulino.

Vesperini, G. 2000. *Poteri Locali*. Rome: Donzelli.

Vinci, I. 2009. "Il Progetto Integrato Territoriale 'Palermo Capitale dell'Euromediterraneo." *Report*. Rome: Formez (Mimeo).

Vinci, I. 2016. "Il dopo-Urban nelle Città Italiane: Storia di un Mainstreaming Interrotto." Working papers. *Urban@it online journal* 2: 1–11. https://www.urbanit.it/wp-content/uploads/2016/10/12_BP_Vinci_I.pdf

Vinci, I. 2017. "EU's Urban Policy from a Southern Perspective: The Case of Palermo." *TRIA. International Journal of Urban Planning* 10 (1): 187–206. doi:10.6092/2281-4574/5317.

Vinci, I. 2019. "Governing the Metropolitan Dimension: A Critical Perspective on Institutional Reshaping and Planning Innovation in Italy." *European Journal of Spatial Development* 70: 1–21. doi:10.30689/EJSD2018:70.1650-9544.

Vinci, I., and S. Di Dio. 2016. "Reshaping the Urban Environment through Mobility Projects and Practices: Lessons from the Case of Palermo." In *Smart Energy in the Smart City. Urban Planning for a Sustainable Future*, edited by R. Papa and R. Fistola, 291–305. Berlin-Heidelberg: Springer. doi:10.1007/978-3-319-31157-9_15.

Index

Allulli, M. 106
Alves, S. 40
analytical framework 32, 77, 79, 106
Andreou, G. 54
Athanassiou, Evangelia 4
Atkinson, R. 32, 34
atypical mega event 62

Balsas, C. J. L. 42
Barca, F. 16
Börzel, T. A. 31
Brundtland Report 59, 70

Cammarata, Diego 108, 112
Carpenter, J. 32
Cavaco, C. 36
changing geography 2, 8
Chrimatistiriou Square 66
Cidades Sustentáveis 2020 35–36
citizen participation 68, 91
city's development process 103, 119–121
climate change 23, 56, 57, 66, 70, 89
Cohesion Policy 2, 6, 8, 9, 16, 17, 19, 21, 23, 30, 77, 79, 82, 83, 87, 91, 94–96, 102
contemporary European cities 3
Costa, C. 43
Costa, J. P. 37
CRUARB 38–40, 42, 46
culture 28, 40, 41, 62, 116

De Gregorio Hurtado, Sonia 3
demographic decline 13, 107
development process 2, 3, 8, 10, 12, 22, 23, 109

ecological modernization 56, 61
economy 55–57
EDUSI 77, 83, 91–96
EEC membership 38
energy 57, 68, 69, 71; efficiency 68, 69, 118
environmental policies 22, 53, 55
environmental protection 55, 56, 58, 60, 61
environmental regeneration 33, 41
EU funded projects 53, 70
EU funded sustainable urban regeneration 61

European Commission 16–18, 30, 43, 60, 75, 76, 83, 92, 95
Europeanisation 3, 4, 29–32, 45, 47, 54, 59, 103; of Portuguese 45; of urban policies 32
European projects 3, 4, 46, 80, 109, 121, 122
European regional development 101
European Regional Policy 6, 56
European sponsored projects 2
European Urban Policies 19, 47
European urban system 14–16, 42
EUROSTAT 2, 7, 9, 12, 15, 18, 108
EU urban policy 3, 17, 18, 20, 22, 55, 70, 75, 77, 103
explicit urban policies 23, 45, 77

financial crisis 4, 35, 54, 59, 60, 69
Florentino, R. 36
funded urban regeneration projects 54

geographies 6, 9, 13
Giannakourou, G. 58
Greek planning system 58, 59
Greenness 65
Green Paper 53, 55–58, 60, 65, 70
Guerra, P. 40

heritage 38, 39, 41, 87

implementation issues 116, 117
iniciativa urbana (IU) programme 77, 80, 83, 87
institutional misfit 58, 61, 72
integrated approach 40, 75, 76, 79, 83–85, 87–90, 93, 94, 96
integrated area-based approaches 30, 31, 39
integrated projects 116, 117, 121, 122
integrated sustainable urban development 30, 35, 91, 102
integrated urban development 17, 34
Italian cities 104, 106, 117, 118
Italian urban policy 103, 105

Karadimitriou, N. 61

Leonardi, R. 30
less developed regions (LDRs) 2, 8–9, 53, 102

Málaga 2, 3, 8, 9, 77, 79–96; EDUSI of 91; URBAN programme in 83
Matkó, M. 102
Medeiros, E. A. 33, 36, 47, 102
mobility revolution 121
Molle, W. 11
municipalities 37, 38, 43, 45, 61, 62, 68, 80, 87, 94, 95, 109, 117, 118, 120–123

New Leipzig Charter 22
New Waterfront 63, 65, 66, 70

Olsen, J. 30
OMAU 89, 90
operational programmes 17, 33, 87, 91, 102
Orlando, Leoluca 108

Pagliuso, A. 36
Pagonis, T. 61
Palermo 2, 3, 8, 9, 101, 102, 107, 108, 111, 112, 114, 117–119, 121
physical interventions 38, 39, 109, 111, 115, 118
pilot projects 33, 62
Pinho, A. 38
Pinho, P. 37
planning reform 60, 72
planning systems 55, 60, 69–72
policy documents 54–56, 58, 60, 62, 69, 70, 76, 79
policy transfer 29, 46
POLIS 33–36, 41, 43
PON Metro project 121 122
PortoVivo 42, 43, 45, 46
Portugal 9, 28, 29, 32, 33, 35–38, 44–47
programming cycles 2, 4, 8, 9, 16, 17, 21, 33–35, 105, 117–120
public–private partnership 121, 122
public spaces 41, 44, 46, 47, 62, 63, 65, 67, 83, 90, 121

Queirós, J. 42

Radaelli, C. 31
regional authorities 7, 16, 17, 20, 69, 105, 118, 120
regional development process 6, 8
regional development programmes 17, 28
regional disparities 6–8, 10, 11, 15, 17, 22
regional operational programmes 34, 102
regional policy 2, 3, 7, 8, 16, 29, 30, 33, 34, 101, 102
rehabilitation 35, 38, 43–45, 67

resilience 56–58, 67, 68, 70, 72
Rio Fernandes, J. 35
Risse, T. 31
Romero, J. 78
Rosa, F. 36
Rossignolo, C. 32

secondary cities 9, 11–13, 15
sectoral investments 32, 34
Seixas, P. C. 37
Sousa, S. 37
Spain 9, 76–80, 82, 83, 87, 88, 90–92
sustainability 54–56, 58, 60–63, 67, 69–72; transferring 53–72
sustainable development 3, 4, 56, 59, 61, 62, 66, 69, 80, 107
sustainable mobility 117–120
Swianiewicz, P. 21

territorial scales 17, 18, 21
Thessaloniki 4, 8, 9, 53–55, 61–65, 68–70, 72
Tortorella, W. 106

URBACT III 57, 67, 68
urban community initiative 16, 30, 75, 78, 80, 81, 83, 87, 104, 119
urban development projects 57, 68, 69
urban enterprise zones 104, 105
urban environment 53–59, 65, 66, 96, 104
urban instruments 79, 80, 82, 92, 94–96
urban interventions 21, 40, 59, 63, 69, 70, 72
urbanism tradition 53, 58, 72
urban policies 2–4, 6, 18, 23, 31, 32, 45–47, 54, 58, 76, 78; change 30
urban priorities 117, 118
URBAN programme 77, 79, 83–86, 90, 91, 93, 96, 115, 117, 118
URBAN I programme 21
URBAN II programme 21, 33, 75, 76, 87, 104, 105
urban projects 20, 34, 55, 68–70, 121
urban regeneration 33–36, 40–46, 54, 58, 61, 63, 70, 77–79, 95; projects 4, 40, 46, 53, 54, 61, 63, 70, 72
urban sustainability 4, 54, 58, 60–62, 70, 77, 82, 120

Van der Zwet, A. 33, 36, 47, 102

waterfront 64, 65, 109, 110